CATS IN HATS

CATS IN HATS

30 GREAT PATTERNS TO KNIT & CROCHET

Sara Thomas

hamlyn

A QUARTO BOOK

An Hachette UK Company
www.hachette.co.uk

First published in Great Britain in 2015
by Hamlyn, a division of
Octopus Publishing Group Ltd
Endeavour House
189 Shaftesbury Avenue
London
WC2H 8JY
www.octopusbooks.co.uk

ISBN 978-0-600-63097-5

A CIP catalogue record for this book is available
from the British Library.

Printed in China by Toppan Leefung

10 9 8 7 6 5 4 3 2 1

Conceived, designed and produced by
Quarto Publishing plc
The Old Brewery
6 Blundell Street
London N7 9BH

QUAR.KCCA

Senior editor: Victoria Lyle
Art editor and designer: Jackie Palmer
Pattern checker: Rachel Vowles
Photographers: Liz Coleman and Phil Wilkins
Illustrator: Kuo Kang Chen
Design assistant: Martina Calvio
Indexer: Helen Snaith
Art director: Caroline Guest
Creative director: Moira Clinch
Publisher: Paul Carslake

CONTENTS

Welcome! 6

Hat Selector 8

KNIT PATTERNS

Dinosaur 10

Bobble Hat 14

Strawberry 16

Pumpkin 20

Sports Cap 22

Spring Chick 24

Punk Mohawk 26

Bunny 30

Turkey 32

Flower Cap 36

I Heart You 38

Extraterrestrial 40

Reindeer Antlers 42

Party Hat 44

Witch 46

Cupcake 48

Banana 50

Santa Hat 52

Elf 56

Top Hat 58

CROCHET PATTERNS

Pompom Hat 62

Little Lion 64

Feline Fox 68

Baby Bear 72

Dog 76

Shark Attack 80

Santa Paws 84

Traffic Cone 88

Unicorn 92

Cowboy Hat 96

TECHNIQUES

Materials and Equipment 100

Knitting Techniques 102

Crochet Techniques 104

Additional Techniques 106

Abbreviations 108

Reading Charts 108

Yarns Used 109

Index 110

Starring 112

WELCOME!

It's very easy for me to pinpoint where my love of cats and knitting came from: my admiration for my grandmother, or 'Nani', as we called her. She lived in a two-storey craftsman-style house in Nashville, Tennessee, with lots of cats and lots of yarn. We'd visit her regularly, and she would regale us with stories of her childhood growing up in Germany. During those tales she'd often be

knitting (continental style), and I was fascinated by the fabric and textures she created, sometimes knitting up a sweater in a weekend. She even sold her designs to local shops and celebrities, as one of many ways to provide for her family of eight. Those weekend visits were full of inspiration for me – often alternating between armfuls of kittens and the many craft supplies my father and Nani encouraged.

As a young adult, I moved to London to study fashion design. Through courses at my university, I became interested in fibre arts. I love the magic that can be created with string and two needles, as well as the history behind this craft.

When I started Scooter Knits on Etsy in March 2009, I was fulfilling a dream six years in the making. My university experience had given me the courage to share things I made with the world. The first cat hat I made was in August 2009, when I adopted my first kitten, Dorothy. After sewing her a tiny T-shirt and making her a tiny house, a tiny hat seemed like the natural next step for this self-professed cat lady. I never imagined when I listed

Sara's cat Dorothy is always first in line to try out the new hats.

my first cat hat on Etsy that it would become the focus of Scooter Knits, but five years later I'm so grateful it did.

My hope is that you will have as much fun making these hats as I've had designing them. I've captured so many great moments of my cats wearing their hats over the years, and I hope you do too! For me, my cats are a special part of my life – not the aloof pets some think them to be, but intelligent animals with unique personalities. This book is an ode to the many sides of our feline friends. Use the patterns in this book to showcase your cat's personality in family photos, on Christmas cards, for Halloween and so on!

We lost my Nani in August 2014, one month before her 92nd birthday. She was intellectual, articulate, loving, talented, quick to put you in your place – an inspiration to me in innumerable ways. This book is dedicated to her.

Sara x

BE KIND TO YOUR FELINE FRIENDS

Some cats are born to model millinery (Gus, Bluebell and Luna, you know who I'm talking about...) and others aren't. If your cat doesn't want to wear your yarn creation, don't force it to.

WORKING THE CATWALK

The models showing off in this book were volunteered because they have exactly the right temperament to wear a hat that looks like a banana, for example.

HAT-WEARING ETIQUETTE

As Lady Mary Crawley might have said, 'A cat should never wear a hat outdoors.' Do not let your cat outside in a hat or leave it to wear a hat unsupervised.

BEHIND THE SCENES! Leeroy reflects on a hard day's work.

Link catnaps between shots.

HAT SELECTOR

KNITTED
HATS

DINOSAUR, PAGE 10

BOBBLE HAT, PAGE 14

STRAWBERRY, PAGE 16

PUMPKIN, PAGE 20

SPORTS CAP, PAGE 22

SPRING CHICK, PAGE 24

PUNK MOHAWK, PAGE 26

BUNNY, PAGE 30

TURKEY, PAGE 32

FLOWER CAP, PAGE 36

I HEART YOU, PAGE 38

EXTRATERRESTRIAL, PAGE 40

REINDEER ANTLERS, PAGE 42

PARTY HAT, PAGE 44

WITCH, PAGE 46

CUPCAKE, PAGE 48

BANANA, PAGE 50

SANTA HAT, PAGE 52

ELF, PAGE 56

TOP HAT, PAGE 58

CROCHET HATS

POMPOM HAT, PAGE 62

LITTLE LION, PAGE 64

FELINE FOX, PAGE 68

BABY BEAR, PAGE 72

DOG, PAGE 76

SHARK ATTACK, PAGE 80

SANTA PAWS, PAGE 84

TRAFFIC CONE, PAGE 88

UNICORN, PAGE 92

COWBOY HAT, PAGE 96

SIZE

TO FIT AN AVERAGE
ADULT CAT

- EAR OPENING: 6 CM (2½ IN.)

- WIDTH OF HAT BETWEEN
  EARS: 6 CM (2½ IN.)

SUPPLIES

- 23 M (25 YD) CHUNKY
  WEIGHT YARN IN A (GREEN)

- 9 M (10 YD) ARAN WEIGHT
  YARN IN B (ORANGE)

- 4.5 MM KNITTING NEEDLES

- 3.75 MM KNITTING NEEDLES

- 3.75 MM CROCHET HOOK

- YARN NEEDLE

FOR THE CAT THAT GOES RAWR! THIS SIMPLE DESIGN
IS GREAT FOR HALLOWEEN, OR ANYTIME!

DINOSAUR

BASE

Using yarn A and 4.5 mm needles, cast on 3 sts, leaving a
64 cm (25 in.) tail.

Row 1: Knit.

Row 2: Kfb, k to last st, kfb. (5 sts)

Rep last 2 rows five more times. (15 sts)

FIRST EAR HOLE

Row 13: K3, cast off next 10 sts, k last st.

Row 14: K2, cast on 10 sts, k3. (The 3 st side is the front
of the hat.)

MIDDLE SECTION

Knit 16 rows.

SECOND EAR HOLE

Row 31: K3, cast off next 10 sts, k last st.

Row 32: K2, cast on 10 sts, k3.

Row 33: Knit.

Row 34: K2tog, k to last 2 sts, k2tog. (13 sts)

Rep last 2 rows five more times. (3 sts)

Cast off, leaving a 64 cm (25 in.) tail.

To create ties, using crochet hook and 64 cm (25 in.) tail,
pull a loop through each stitch on cast off edge (3 loops),
yo, pull one loop through, work 25ch, pull end through
loop tightly and snip extra yarn. Repeat with other 64 cm
(25 in.) tail.

LEEROY MODELS THE DINOSAUR HAT WHILE
PLAYING WITH HIS DINOSAUR MODELS.

SPIKES
(Make 3)
Using yarn B and 3.75 mm needles, cast on 8 sts.
Rows 1–3: Knit.
Row 4: K2tog, k4, k2tog. (6 sts)
Rows 5–7: Knit.
Row 8: K2tog, k2, k2tog. (4 sts)
Row 9: Knit.
Row 10: [K2tog] twice. (2 sts)
Row 11: K2tog.
Fasten off, leaving a 15 cm (6 in.) tail.

ASSEMBLY
Turn the spikes so that the cast on and cast off tails are at the bottom. You will have three dinosaur shaped spikes. The lower edge with both tails is the edge you sew to the hat base.

Starting at the centre front of the base, stitch the lower edge of the first spike into place. Weave in both ends to underside of hat and secure. Repeat with other spikes, following centre of hat and stitching into lower edge.

SPIKES: 4 X 4 CM
(1½ X 1½ IN.)

SKILL LEVEL: BEGINNER

SIZE

TO FIT A SMALL
ADULT CAT
- EAR OPENING: 5 CM
  (2 IN.)
- WIDTH OF HAT BETWEEN
  EARS: 5 CM (2 IN.)

SUPPLIES

- 18 M (20 YD) ARAN
  WEIGHT YARN IN A
  (BLUE)
- 4.5 M (5 YD) ARAN
  WEIGHT YARN IN B (RED)
- 4.5 MM KNITTING
  NEEDLES
- YARN NEEDLE
- POMPOM MAKER
  (OPTIONAL)

DOES YOUR CAT GET FRISKY ABOUT COLDER WEATHER?
THEN HE MIGHT APPRECIATE THIS CLASSIC WINTER STYLE,
WITH A CATTY TWIST!

BOBBLE HAT

BASE
Using yarn A, cast on 3 sts,
leaving a 25 cm (10 in.) tail.
Row 1: Knit.
Row 2: Kfb, k to last st, kfb.
(5 sts)
Rep last 2 rows five more
times. (15 sts)
FIRST EAR HOLE
Row 13: K3, cast off next
10 sts, k last st.
Row 14: K2, cast on 10 sts,
k3. (The 3 st side is the front
of the hat.)
MIDDLE SECTION
Knit 16 rows.
SECOND EAR HOLE
Row 31: K3, bind off
next 10 sts, k last st.
Row 32: K2, cast on
10 sts, k3.
Row 33: Knit.
Row 34: K2tog, k to
last 2 sts, k2tog. (13 sts)
Rep last 2 rows five more
times. (3 sts)
Cast off, leaving a 25 cm
(10 in.) tail.

POMPOM: 2.5 CM
(1 IN.) DIAMETER

BRAIDED TRIM:
66 CM (26 IN.)
TOTAL LENGTH

BRAIDED TRIM

Cut 3 x 91 cm (36 in.) pieces from both
yarns A and B (6 strands total). Holding
strands together, knot approximately 2.5 cm
(1 in.) from top. Working with three pairs
of A and B strands, make a 3-ply braid until
trim measures 66 cm (26 in.). Knot, and trim
tassel lengths. Stitch to the front edge of base,
using cast on and cast off tails to sew into
place. Centre trim to the centre of the hat.
You should be left with approximately

LUNA CHECKS THE WEATHER TO SEE IF IT'S WORTH
LEAVING HER COSY DEN IN ORDER TO PLAY OUTSIDE.

19 cm (7½ in.) ties on both sides. Weave
tails into the underside of the hat and snip.
Make a 2.5 cm (1 in.) pompom from yarns
A and B, and attach to the centre of the base.
Now enjoy, take lots of pictures and give
your sweet cat a treat for being such a
handsome model!

METHOD: KNIT

SKILL LEVEL: BEGINNER

SIZE

TO FIT AN AVERAGE
ADULT CAT
- EAR OPENING: 6 CM
  (2½ IN.)
- WIDTH OF HAT BETWEEN
  EARS: 6 CM (2½ IN.)

✳ ✳ ✳ ✳ ✳

SUPPLIES

- 23 M (25 YD) ARAN
  WEIGHT YARN IN A (RED)
- 9 M (10 YD) ARAN
  WEIGHT YARN IN B (GREEN)
- 2.7 M (3 YD) ARAN
  WEIGHT YARN IN C (WHITE)
- 4.5 MM KNITTING
  NEEDLES
- 3.75 MM DPNS
- 3.75 MM CROCHET HOOK
- YARN NEEDLE

A KITSCHY SUMMER DESIGN! YOU CAN LEAVE THE SEEDS OFF THE DESIGN AND IT WILL DOUBLE AS A TOMATO.

STRAWBERRY

BASE
Using yarn A and 4.5 mm needles, cast on 3 sts, leaving a 64 cm (25 in.) tail.
Row 1: Knit.
Row 2: Kfb, k to last st, kfb. (5 sts)
Rep last 2 rows four more times. (13 sts)
FIRST EAR HOLE
Row 11: K2, cast off next 9 sts, k last st.
Row 12: K2, cast on 9 sts, k2.
MIDDLE SECTION
Knit 16 rows.
SECOND EAR HOLE
Row 29: K2, cast off next 9 sts, k last st.
Row 30: K2, cast on 9 sts, k2.
Row 31: Knit.
Row 32: K2tog, k to last 2 sts, k2tog. (11 sts)
Rep last 2 rows four more times. (3 sts)
Cast off, leaving a 64 cm (25 in.) tail.

To create ties, using crochet hook and 64 cm (25 in.) tail, pull a loop through each stitch on cast off edge (3 loops), yo, pull one loop through, work 25ch, pull end through loop tightly and snip extra yarn. Repeat with other 64 cm (25 in.) tail.

STEM

Using yarn B and two 3.75 mm dpns, cast on 4 sts and knit a row. Do not turn needle. Slide the 4 sts to other end of needle, bring yarn around from the back and knit the 4 sts again. This forms the i-cord technique. Knit in i-cord technique, until stem measures 5 cm (2 in.). You may find it helpful to pull on the cast on edge after every few rows to help the shape. Once complete, snip a 25 cm (10 in.) tail and pull through all 4 loops on the needle. Weave cast off tail through to bottom of stem. You will use this tail to stitch the stem to the base.

LEAVES
(Make 3)

Using yarn B and two 3.75 mm dpns, cast on 5 sts.
Rows 1–2: Knit.
Row 3: K2tog, k1, k2tog. (3 sts)
Row 4: Knit.
Row 5: K2tog, k1. (2 sts)
Row 6: K2tog.
Fasten off, leaving a 15 cm (6 in.) tail. Weave through sides of leaf to cast on edge.

STEM: 5 CM
(2 IN.) I-CORD

SEEDS:
STITCHES
IN YARN C

ASSEMBLY

Using the cast off tail from the stem, stitch it onto the centre of the base. Stitch securely around the cast on edges of the stem. Once complete, pull the cast on and cast off stem tails to the underside of the hat and secure.

Attach leaves to the base of the hat, around the bottom of the stem, by stitching through the cast on edge of the leaves. Use the longer tail to stitch. Weave all ends to the underside of hat and secure.

To finish the hat, thread yarn needle with yarn C. Make short, well-placed stitches on the base of the hat to represent the seeds. Do not do too many – use the photo for reference if necessary. Secure yarn to the underside of the hat.

SKILL LEVEL: BEGINNER

SIZE

TO FIT AN AVERAGE
ADULT CAT

- EAR OPENING: 6 CM
  (2½ IN.)
- WIDTH OF HAT BETWEEN
  EARS: 6 CM (2½ IN.)

✳ ✳ ✳ ✳ ✳

SUPPLIES

- 23 M (25 YD) ARAN
  WEIGHT YARN IN A
  (ORANGE)
- 9 M (10 YD) ARAN
  WEIGHT YARN IN B
  (GREEN)
- 4.5 MM KNITTING
  NEEDLES
- 3.75 MM DPNS
- 3.75 MM CROCHET HOOK
- YARN NEEDLE

FOR YOUR LITTLE PURR PUMPKIN! KNIT THIS IN A
VARIETY OF AUTUMN COLOURS FOR ALL THE LITTLE
PUMPKINS IN YOUR PATCH.

PUMPKIN

STEM: 5 CM
(2 IN.) I-CORD

BASE

Using yarn A and 4.5 mm needles,
cast on 3 sts, leaving a 64 cm
(25 in.) tail.
Row 1: Knit.
Row 2: Kfb, k to last st, kfb.
(5 sts)
Rep last 2 rows four more times.
(13 sts)
FIRST EAR HOLE
Row 11: K2, cast off next 9 sts,
k last st.
Row 12: K2, cast on 9 sts, k2.
MIDDLE SECTION
Knit 16 rows.
SECOND EAR HOLE
Row 29: K2, cast off next
9 sts, k last st.
Row 30: K2, cast on 9 sts, k2.
Row 31: Knit.
Row 32: K2tog, k to last 2 sts,
k2tog. (11 sts)
Rep last 2 rows four more
times. (3 sts)
Cast off, leaving a 25 in.
(64 cm) tail.

To create ties, using crochet hook and 64 cm (25 in.) tail, pull a
loop through each stitch on cast off edge (3 loops), yo, pull one
loop through, work 25ch, pull end through loop tightly and snip
extra yarn. Repeat with other 64 cm (25 in.) tail.

STEM

Using yarn B and two 3.75 mm dpns, cast on 4 sts and knit a
row. Do not turn needle. Slide the 4 sts to other end of needle,
bring yarn around from the back and knit the 4 sts again. This
forms the i-cord technique.

Knit i-cord, until stem measures 5 cm (2 in.). You may find it helpful to pull on the cast on edge after every few rows to help the shape. Once complete, snip a 25 cm (10 in.) tail and pull through all 4 loops on the needle. Weave cast off tail through to bottom of stem. You will use this tail to stitch the stem to the base.

ASSEMBLY

Using the cast off tail from the stem, stitch it onto the centre of the base. Stitch securely around the cast on edges of the stem. Once complete, pull the cast on and cast off stem tails to the underside of the hat and secure.

LEEROY BASKS IN THE AUTUMN SUNLIGHT IN THE PUMPKIN HAT.

TENSIONS ARE HIGH AS LUNA WATCHES THE CLOSING
MOMENTS OF THE BASEBALL GAME.

SIZE

TO FIT A SMALL
ADULT CAT

• EAR OPENING: 5 CM (2 IN.)
• WIDTH OF HAT BETWEEN
EARS: 5 CM (2 IN.)

SUPPLIES

• 14 M (15 YD) ARAN WEIGHT
YARN IN A (RED)
• 14 M (15 YD) ARAN
WEIGHT YARN IN B (WHITE)
• 14 M (15 YD) ARAN
WEIGHT YARN IN C (BLUE)
• 4.5 MM KNITTING NEEDLES
• 4 MM CROCHET HOOK
• YARN NEEDLE

KNIT THIS QUICK PROJECT UP IN YOUR FAVOURITE
SPORTS TEAM COLOURS!

SPORTS CAP

BASE
Using yarn A, cast on 3 sts,
leaving a 64 cm (25 in.) tail.
Row 1: Knit.
Row 2: Kfb, k to last st, kfb.
(5 sts)
Rep last 2 rows five more
times. (15 sts)
FIRST EAR HOLE
Row 13: K2, cast off next
11 sts, k last st.
Row 14: K2, cast on 11 sts,
k2.
MIDDLE SECTION
Knit 1 row.
Change to yarn B.
Knit 14 rows.
Change to yarn C.
Knit 1 row.
SECOND EAR HOLE
Row 31: K2, cast off next 11 sts,
k last st.
Row 32: K2, cast on 11 sts, k2.
Row 33: Knit.
Row 34: K2tog, k to last 2 sts, k2tog. (13 sts)
Rep last 2 rows five more times. (3 sts)
Cast off, leaving a 64 cm (25 in.) tail.

To create ties, using crochet hook and 64 cm (25 in.)
tail, pull a loop through each stitch on cast off edge
(3 loops), yo, pull one loop through, work 25ch, pull
end through loop tightly and snip extra yarn. Repeat
with other 64 cm (25 in.) tail.

BRIM: 5 CM
(2 IN.) WIDE

MAKE SURE TO CHOOSE A TEXTURED YARN FOR THIS PROJECT — IT MAKES ALL THE DIFFERENCE IN ACHIEVING AN ULTRA-FLUFFY CHICK!

SPRING CHICK

SIZE

TO FIT AN AVERAGE ADULT CAT

- EAR OPENING: 6 CM (2½ IN.)
- WIDTH OF HAT BETWEEN EARS: 6 CM (2½ IN.)

SUPPLIES

- 23 M (25 YD) FAUX FUR YARN IN A (YELLOW)
- 9 M (10 YD) ARAN WEIGHT YARN IN B (BLACK)
- 9 M (10 YD) ARAN WEIGHT YARN IN C (ORANGE)
- 5 MM KNITTING NEEDLES
- 4 MM CROCHET HOOK
- YARN NEEDLE

EYES: 2 CM
(¾ IN.) DIAMETER

BEAK:
6 X 5 CM
(2½ X 2 IN.)

BASE

Using yarn A, cast on 3 sts, leaving a 64 cm
(25 in.) tail.

Row 1: Knit.

Row 2: Kfb, k to last st, kfb. (5 sts)

Rep last 2 rows five more times. (15 sts)

FIRST EAR HOLE

Row 13: K2, cast off next 11 sts, k last st.

Row 14: K2, cast on 11 sts, k2.

MIDDLE SECTION

Knit 16 rows.

SECOND EAR HOLE

Row 31: K2, cast off next 11 sts, k last st.

Row 32: K2, cast on 11 sts, k2.

Row 33: Knit.

Row 34: K2tog, k to last 2 sts, k2tog. (13 sts)

Rep last 2 rows five more times. (3 sts)

Cast off, leaving a 64 cm (25 in.) tail.

To create ties, using crochet hook and 64 cm
(25 in.) tail, pull a loop through each stitch
on cast off edge (3 loops), yo, pull one loop
through, work 25ch, pull end through loop
tightly and snip extra yarn. Repeat with other
64 cm (25 in.) tail.

GRACIE STRIKES A POSE TO MODEL
THE SPRING CHICK HAT.

EYES
(Make 2)

Using yarn B and crochet hook, make
a magic ring.

Rnd 1: 1ch, 6dc in ring, sl st in first ch.

Rnd 2: 1ch, [2dc in first st, 1dc] 3 times,
sl st in first dc.

Fasten off, leaving an 18 cm (7 in.) tail.

BEAK

Using yarn C, cast on 12 sts, leaving
a 25 cm (10 in.) tail.

Rows 1–2: Knit.

Row 3: K2tog, k8, k2tog. (10 sts)

Row 4: Knit.

Row 5: K2tog, k6, k2tog. (8 sts)

Row 6: Knit.

Row 7: K2tog, k4, k2tog. (6 sts)

Rows 8–9: Knit.

Row 10: K2tog, k2, k2tog. (4 sts)

Row 11: Knit.

Row 12: [K2tog] twice. (2 sts)

Cast off, leaving a 15 cm (6 in.) tail.

ASSEMBLY

BEAK

Lay the beak so that both the cast on and
cast off tails are upright. This is the top of the
beak. Place beak, top side up, along the front
of the base, in the middle and about 1 cm
(½ in.) from edge (either side can be the front
of the hat). Using the 25 cm (10 in.) tail and
a yarn needle, stitch along the edges of the
beak that are lying on the hat. Also use the
15 cm (6 in.) tail. Attach securely.

EYES

Place eyes so that they are just above the top
of the beak, evenly spaced. Attach securely
with yarn tails and yarn needle.

METHOD: KNIT

SKILL LEVEL: INTERMEDIATE

SIZE

TO FIT AN AVERAGE
ADULT CAT

• EAR OPENING: 6 CM
(2½ IN.)

• WIDTH OF HAT BETWEEN
EARS: 6 CM (2½ IN.)

✳ ✳ ✳ ✳ ✳

SUPPLIES

• 23 M (25 YD) ARAN
WEIGHT YARN IN A (BLACK)

• 14 M (15 YD) CHUNKY
WEIGHT YARN IN B (PINK)

• 4.5 MM KNITTING NEEDLES

• 4 MM CROCHET HOOK

• YARN NEEDLE

FOR THE ULTIMATE ANARCHIST IN YOUR FAMILY,
KNIT A PUNK ROCKER FAUX HAWK IN SHOCKING PINK!

PUNK MOHAWK

BASE

Using yarn A, cast on 3 sts, leaving a 25 in.
(64 cm) tail.
Row 1: Knit.
Row 2: Kfb, k to last st, kfb. (5 sts)
Rep last 2 rows five more times. (15 sts)

FIRST EAR HOLE

Row 13: K3, cast off next 10 sts, k last st.
Row 14: K2, cast on 10 sts, k3. (The 3 st side
is the front of the hat.)

MIDDLE SECTION

Knit 16 rows.

SECOND EAR HOLE

Row 31: K3, cast off next 10 sts, k last st.
Row 32: K2, cast on 10 sts, k3.
Row 33: Knit.
Row 34: K2tog, k to last 2 sts, k2tog. (13 sts)
Rep last 2 rows five more times. (3 sts)
Cast off, leaving a 64 cm (25 in.) tail.

Using crochet hook, work 25ch on each side using
the 64 cm (25 in.) tails left at the beginning and
end of your work. This creates the ties for your
cat hat.

FAUX HAWK

Using yarn B, clip fifteen to twenty 5 cm (2 in.)
pieces. You will attach these pieces to the centre
garter stitch ridge of your cat hat base.

ASSEMBLY

You will attach the faux hawk pieces in a manner similar to attaching fringing to a scarf. To attach, slide crochet hook underneath the first stitch in the centre garter stitch ridge on the base of the hat. Take a 5 cm (2 in.) piece of yarn, fold it in half and pull the loop through the garter row using the crochet hook. Take the ends of the faux hawk yarn and pull them through the loop so that it is securely knotted. The faux hawk yarn should stand upright using this method. Repeat, cutting more 5 cm (2 in.) pieces if necessary, and continue attaching them down the centre garter stitch row.

To create a fuller faux hawk, clip more yarn and attach it to both sides of the centre garter stitch ridge. When finished, trim faux hawk to a uniform length (about 2.5 cm/1 in.).

FAUX HAWK PIECES:
5 CM (2 IN.) LONG

JASPER PACES THE PAVEMENT WITH PRIDE IN HIS PUNK MOHAWK HAT.

SKILL LEVEL: INTERMEDIATE

SIZE

TO FIT AN AVERAGE
ADULT CAT

• EAR OPENING: 6 CM
  (2½ IN.)

• WIDTH OF HAT BETWEEN
  EARS: 6 CM (2½ IN.)

✳ ✳ ✳ ✳ ✳

SUPPLIES

• 37 M (40 YD) ARAN
  WEIGHT YARN IN CREAM

• 4.5 MM KNITTING
  NEEDLES

• 4 MM CROCHET HOOK

• YARN NEEDLE

IF YOUR EARS HANG LOW, THIS BUNNY HAT WILL BE THE PERFECT FIT!

BUNNY

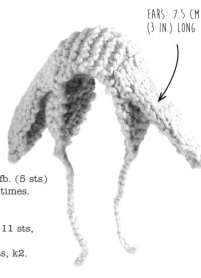

EARS: 7.5 CM
(3 IN.) LONG

BASE
Cast on 3 sts, leaving
a 64 cm (25 in.) tail.
Row 1: Knit.
Row 2: Kfb, k to last st, kfb. (5 sts)
Rep last 2 rows five more times.
(15 sts)

FIRST EAR HOLE
Row 13: K2, cast off next 11 sts,
k last st.
Row 14: K2, cast on 11 sts, k2.

MIDDLE SECTION
Knit 16 rows.

SECOND EAR HOLE
Row 31: K2, cast off next 11 sts, k last st.
Row 32: K2, cast on 11 sts, k2.
Row 33: Knit.
Row 34: K2tog, k to last 2 sts, k2tog. (13 sts)
Rep last 2 rows five more times. (3 sts)
Cast off, leaving a 64 cm (25 in.) tail.

To create ties, using crochet hook and 64 cm (25 in.)
tail, pull a loop through each stitch on cast off edge
(3 loops), yo, pull one loop through, work 25ch, pull
end through loop tightly and snip extra yarn. Repeat
with other 64 cm (25 in.) tail.

EARS
(Make 2)
Cast on 13 sts, leaving a 25 cm (10 in.) tail
(you will use this tail to attach the ear to the
base of the hat later).
Row 1: Knit.
Row 2: Purl.
Rep last 2 rows once more.
Row 5: K1, k2tog, k7, k2tog, k1. (11 sts)
Row 6: Purl.

Row 7: Knit.
Row 8: Purl.
Rep last 2 rows three
more times.
Row 15: K1, k2tog, k5,
k2tog, k1. (9 sts)
Row 16: Purl.
Row 17: Knit.
Row 18: Purl.
Row 19: K1, k2tog, k3,
k2tog, k1. (7 sts)
Row 20: Purl.
Row 21: K1, k2tog, k1,
k2tog, k1. (5 sts)
Row 22: Purl.
Cast off, leaving a 15 cm
(6 in.) tail.

Using yarn needle,
weave in cast off tail.
Adjust the ear length in
this pattern by increasing
(or decreasing) between
Rows 7 and 14.

ASSEMBLY
To attach ears, use cast on
tail and yarn needle to stitch
one ear to the middle section
of the base, centred above ear
opening and with knit side
uppermost. Secure both ends
around ear opening (so that
ear is slightly curved down).
Stitch the ear along the cast
on edge, placing it on the
first garter row above the ear
opening. Repeat with second
ear and other ear opening.

WHO IS THIS HANDSOME
FURBALL? IT'S HUCK
MODELLING THE BUNNY HAT.

SKILL LEVEL: INTERMEDIATE

SIZE

TO FIT AN AVERAGE
ADULT CAT

- EAR OPENING: 6 CM (2½ IN.)
- WIDTH OF HAT BETWEEN
  EARS: 6 CM (2½ IN.)

✳ ✳ ✳ ✳ ✳

SUPPLIES

- 23 M (25 YD) CHUNKY
  WEIGHT YARN IN A (BROWN)
- 9 M (10 YD) ARAN WEIGHT
  YARN IN B (RED)
- 9 M (10 YD) ARAN WEIGHT
  YARN IN C (BLACK)
- 14 M (15 YD) ARAN WEIGHT
  YARN IN D (ORANGE)
- 9 M (10 YD) ARAN WEIGHT
  YARN IN E (WHITE)
- 4.5 MM KNITTING NEEDLES
- 4 MM CROCHET HOOK
- YARN NEEDLE

THE CUTEST LITTLE TURKEY
YOU EVER DID SEE!

TURKEY

BASE
Using yarn A, cast on 3 sts, leaving a 15 cm (6 in.) tail.
Row 1: Knit.
Row 2: Kfb, k to last st, kfb. (5 sts)
Rep last 2 rows five more times. (15 sts)
FIRST EAR HOLE
Row 13: K2, cast off next 11 sts, k last st.
Row 14: K2, cast on 11 sts, k2.
MIDDLE SECTION
Knit 16 rows.
SECOND EAR HOLE
Row 31: K2, cast off next 11 sts, k last st.
Row 32: K2, cast on 11 sts, k2.
Row 33: Knit.
Row 34: K2tog, k to last 2 sts, k2tog. (13 sts)
Rep last 2 rows five more times. (3 sts)
Cast off, leaving a 15 cm (6 in.) tail.

To create ties, cut two pieces of yarn B measuring 76 cm
(30 in.) each. Using crochet hook and one piece of yarn, pull
a loop through the end of the base and work 25ch. Pull yarn
through last loop tightly and trim. Weave in starting end to
underside of the hat. Repeat on other side.

OUTER EYES
(Make 2)
Using yarn E and crochet hook, make a magic ring.
Rnd 1: 1ch, 12dc in ring, sl st in first ch.
Rnd 2: 1ch, [2dc in first st, 1dc] 6 times, sl st in first dc.
Cut yarn, leaving a 25 cm (10 in.) tail, and pull tightly
through loop.

INNER EYES
(Make 2)
Using yarn C and crochet hook, make a magic ring.

Rnd 1: 1ch, 6dc in ring, sl st in first ch.
Rnd 2: 1ch, [2dc in first st, 1dc] 3 times, sl st in first dc.

Cut yarn, leaving an 18 cm (7 in.) tail, and pull tightly through loop.

BEAK
Using yarn D, cast on 12 sts, leaving a 25 cm (10 in.) tail.

Rows 1–2: Knit.
Row 3: K2tog, k8, k2tog. (10 sts)
Row 4: Knit.
Row 5: K2tog, k6, k2tog. (8 sts)
Row 6: Knit.
Row 7: K2tog, k4, k2tog. (6 sts)
Rows 8–9: Knit.
Row 10: K2tog, k2, k2tog. (4 sts)
Row 11: Knit.
Row 12: [K2tog] twice. (2 sts)
Cast off, leaving a 15 cm (6 in.) tail.

ASSEMBLY
BEAK
Lay the beak so that both the cast on and cast off tails are upright. This is the top of the beak. Place beak, top side up, along the front of the base, in the middle and about 1 cm (½ in.) from edge (either side can be the front of the hat). Using the 25 cm (10 in.) tail and a yarn needle, stitch along the edges of the beak that are lying on the hat. Also use the 15 cm (6 in.) tail. Attach securely.
EYES
Place eyes so that they are touching the top of the beak, evenly spaced. Attach securely with yarn tails and yarn needle.

GOBBLE
Using yarn B and crochet hook, pull a loop through base at the centre of the stitched on edge of the beak. Work 7ch through the beak and base using photo as guide, work 3ch and cut yarn. Weave end through ch sts and to underside of hat.

OUTER EYES:
2.5 X 4 CM
(1 X 1½ IN.)

GOBBLE:
5 CM (2 IN.)

BEAK:
5 X 5 CM
(2 X 2 IN.)

LYRIC PLAYFULLY MODELS
THE TURKEY HAT.

METHOD: KNIT

SKILL LEVEL: INTERMEDIATE

SIZE

TO FIT AN AVERAGE
ADULT CAT

- EAR OPENING: 6 CM (2½ IN.)
- WIDTH OF HAT BETWEEN
  EARS: 5 CM (2 IN.)

SUPPLIES

- 37 M (40 YD) ARAN WEIGHT
  YARN IN A (RED)
- 9 M (10 YD) ARAN WEIGHT
  YARN IN B (BLUE)
- 4.5 MM KNITTING NEEDLES
- 3.75 MM KNITTING NEEDLES
- 4 MM CROCHET HOOK
- YARN NEEDLE

FOR ALL THOSE COOL CATS OUT THERE IN STYLISH HATS: PUT
A FLOWER IN YOUR CAP FOR A SPECIAL FELINE FLOURISH!

FLOWER CAP

BASE

Using yarn A and 4.5 mm
needles, cast on 3 sts, leaving
a 15 cm (6 in.) tail.
Row 1: Knit.
Row 2: Kfb, k to last st, kfb.
(5 sts)
Rep last 2 rows five more times.
(15 sts)
FIRST EAR HOLE
Row 13: K2, cast off next
11 sts, k last st.
Row 14: K2, cast on 11 sts, k2.
MIDDLE SECTION
Knit 16 rows.
SECOND EAR HOLE
Row 31: K2, cast off next
11 sts, k last st.
Row 32: K2, cast on 11 sts, k2.
Row 33: Knit.
Row 34: K2tog, k to last 2 sts,
k2tog. (13 sts)
Rep last 2 rows five more times. (3 sts)
Cast off, leaving a 15 cm (6 in.) tail.

FLOWER: 2 CM
(¾ IN.) DIAMETER

BRIM: 10 CM
(4 IN.) WIDE

To create ties, cut two pieces of yarn A measuring 76 cm (30 in.)
each. Using crochet hook and one piece of yarn, pull a loop
through the end of the base and work 25ch. Pull yarn through
last loop tightly and trim. Weave in starting end to underside of
the hat. Repeat on other side.

BRIM

Using yarn A and 3.75 mm needles, pick up 12 sts along front of base, starting in front of one ear hole and picking them up evenly until you work your way past the second ear hole. Knit 1 row.

Row 2: Kfb of each st. (24 sts)
Rows 3–5: Knit.
Row 6: Kfb, k to last st, kfb. (26 sts)
Cast off using yarn B.
Thread ends down the sides of the brim and secure to the underside of the base.

VARIATION

Use yarn B to knit base, yarn A for brim and cast off brim with yarn B.

THESE COMPLEMENTARY FLOWER CAPS ARE MODELLED BY LYRIC AND LINK.

FLOWER

Using yarn B and crochet hook, make a magic ring.

Rnd 1: 1ch, 6dc in ring, sl st in first ch.
Rnd 2: [2dc in first st, 1dc] 3 times. Change to yarn A.
Rnd 3: Dc in each st, sl st in first dc.
Cut yarn and pull through loop. Weave in end to centre. Attach to the right of the brim.

SHOW YOUR CAT SOME LOVE WITH THIS ADORABLE HEART HAT.

I HEART YOU

METHOD: KNIT

SKILL LEVEL: INTERMEDIATE

SIZE

TO FIT AN AVERAGE
ADULT CAT

- EAR OPENING: 6 CM
  (2½ IN.)

- WIDTH OF HAT BETWEEN
  EARS: 6 CM (2½ IN.)

✳✳✳✳✳

SUPPLIES

- 23 M (25 YD) ARAN WEIGHT
  YARN IN A (BROWN)

- 4.5 M (5 YD) ARAN WEIGHT
  YARN IN B (RED)

- 4.5 MM DPNS

- 4 MM CROCHET HOOK

- 1 X 15 CM (6 IN.) PIECE OF
  PIPE CLEANER (PREFERABLY
  IN A CORRESPONDING
  COLOUR TO YOUR YARN)

- YARN NEEDLE

BASE

Using yarn A and two dpns, cast on
3 sts, leaving a 64 cm (25 in.) tail.
Row 1: Knit.
Row 2: Kfb, k to last st, kfb. (5 sts)
Rep last 2 rows five more times. (15 sts)
FIRST EAR HOLE
Row 13: K3, cast off next 10 sts, k last st.
Row 14: K2, cast on 10 sts, k3. (The 3 st
side is the front of the hat.)
MIDDLE SECTION
Knit 16 rows.
SECOND EAR HOLE
Row 31: K3, cast off next 10 sts,
k last st.
Row 32: K2, cast on 10 sts, k3.
Row 33: Knit.
Row 34: K2tog, k to last 2 sts, k2tog. (13 sts)
Rep last 2 rows five more times. (3 sts)
Cast off, leaving a 64 cm (25 in.) tail.

Using crochet hook, work 25ch on each side using the
64 cm (25 in.) tails left at the beginning and end of your
work. This creates the ties for your cat hat.

HEART

Using yarn B and two dpns, cast on 4 sts, leaving a 15 cm
(6 in.) tail. Knit a row. Do not turn needle. Holding piece
of pipe cleaner in place, slide the 4 sts to other end of
needle, bring yarn around from the back, encasing the
pipe cleaner, and knit the 4 sts again. This forms the
i-cord technique. Using the i-cord method, knit around
pipe cleaner until only 0.5 cm (¼ in.) of pipe cleaner
remains exposed at both ends. Cut yarn, leaving a 15 cm
(6 in.) tail, and use yarn needle to pull tail through sts on
needle. Bend the i-cord into a heart shape.

ASSEMBLY

Using a knitting needle as a guide, poke both ends
of the heart through the centre of the hat base. Bring
the exposed ends back up through the base and twist
them around themselves securely. Using a yarn
needle, stitch the base of the heart to the base of
the hat. Stitch so that the pipe cleaner is no longer
exposed and the heart sits upright. Pull both tails
through to underside of hat, and knot the ends to
anchor the heart.

WHO CAN RESIST THE LOVING
LOOK OF PERCY?

IT'S AN ENCOUNTER OF THE THIRD KIND! KNITTING AROUND A FLEXIBLE PIPE CLEANER ALLOWS YOUR CAT'S THIRD EYE TO PEER IN WHATEVER DIRECTION YOU CHOOSE.

EXTRATERRESTRIAL

BASE

Using yarn A and 4.5 mm needles, cast on 3 sts, leaving a 64 cm (25 in.) tail.
Row 1: Knit.
Row 2: Kfb, k to last st, kfb. (5 sts)
Rep last 2 rows five more times. (15 sts)
FIRST EAR HOLE
Row 13: K2, cast off next 11 sts, k last st.
Row 14: K2, cast on 11 sts, k2.
MIDDLE SECTION
Knit 16 rows.
SECOND EAR HOLE
Row 31: K2, cast off next 11 sts, k last st.
Row 32: K2, cast on 11 sts, k2.
Row 33: Knit.
Row 34: K2tog, k to last 2 sts, k2tog. (13 sts)
Rep last 2 rows five more times. (3 sts)
Cast off, leaving a 64 cm (25 in.) tail.

To create ties, using crochet hook and 64 cm (25 in.) tail, pull a loop through each stitch on cast off edge (3 loops), yo, pull one loop through, work 25ch, pull end through loop tightly and snip extra yarn. Repeat with other 64 cm (25 in.) tail.

EYE

Using yarn A and two 3.25 mm dpns, cast on 4 sts, leaving a 38 cm (15 in.) tail. Knit a row. Do not turn needle. Holding piece of pipe cleaner in place, slide the 4 sts to other end of needle, bring yarn around from the back, encasing the pipe cleaner, and knit the 4 sts again. This forms the i-cord

technique. Using the i-cord method, knit around pipe cleaner until it is enclosed, leaving 1 cm (½ in.) exposed at the bottom.
Next row: Kfb of each st. (8 sts)
Divide sts onto three dpns and join to work in the round.
Next rnd: Kfb of each st. (16 sts)
Knit 3 rnds.
Next rnd: K2tog around. (8 sts)
Lightly stuff with fibre filling.
Next rnd: K2tog around. (4 sts)
Cut yarn and pull through remaining loops. Weave in end.

Using yarn B and yarn needle, sew several long stitches on centre of eyeball to create a pupil. Weave in ends.

ASSEMBLY

Centre the eye on the base. Poke the exposed pipe cleaner through the base, using a knitting needle as a guide. Bring the exposed end back up through the base and twist it around itself securely. Using a yarn needle and the cast on tail of the i-cord, stitch the eye to the base along the cast on edge of the i-cord. Pull both tails through to underside of the hat, and knot the ends to anchor the eye.

EYE: 7.5 CM (3 IN.) PIPE CLEANER COVERED IN I-CORD

METHOD: KNIT

SKILL LEVEL: INTERMEDIATE

SIZE

TO FIT AN AVERAGE
ADULT CAT

- EAR OPENING: 6 CM
  (2½ IN.)
- WIDTH OF HAT BETWEEN
  EARS: 6 CM (2½ IN.)

SUPPLIES

- 32 M (35 YD) ARAN
  WEIGHT YARN IN A (GREEN)
- SCRAP OF ARAN WEIGHT
  YARN IN B (BLACK)
- 4.5 MM KNITTING NEEDLES
- 3.25 MM DPNS
- 4 MM CROCHET HOOK
- 1 X 7.5 CM (3 IN.) PIECE
  OF PIPE CLEANER
  (PREFERABLY IN A
  CORRESPONDING COLOUR
  TO YOUR YARN)
- YARN NEEDLE
- POLYESTER FIBRE FILLING

ANTLERS ARE THE PERFECT HOLIDAY GIFT, GUARANTEED TO INSPIRE SOME HOLIDAY CHEER IN YOUR FAVOURITE FELINE!

REINDEER ANTLERS

METHOD: KNIT

SKILL LEVEL: INTERMEDIATE

SIZE

TO FIT A SMALL ADULT CAT

- EAR OPENING: 5 CM (2 IN.)
- WIDTH OF HAT BETWEEN EARS: 5 CM (2 IN.)

SUPPLIES

- 27 M (30 YD) ARAN WEIGHT YARN
- 4.5 MM DPNS
- 2 X 10 CM (4 IN.) PIECES OF PIPE CLEANER (PREFERABLY IN A CORRESPONDING COLOUR TO YOUR YARN)
- 4 MM CROCHET HOOK
- YARN NEEDLE

BASE

Using two dpns, cast on 3 sts, leaving a
64 cm (25 in.) tail.

Row 1: Knit.

Row 2: Kfb, k to last st, kfb. (5 sts)

Rep last 2 rows five more times. (15 sts)

FIRST EAR HOLE

Row 13: K3, cast off next 10 sts, k last st.

Row 14: K2, cast on 10 sts, k3. (The 3 st side
is the front of the hat.)

MIDDLE SECTION

Knit 16 rows.

SECOND EAR HOLE

Row 31: K3, cast off next 10 sts, k last st.

Row 32: K2, cast on 10 sts, k3.

Row 33: Knit.

Row 34: K2tog, k to last 2 sts, k2tog. (13 sts)

Rep last 2 rows five more times. (3 sts)

Cast off, leaving a 64 cm (25 in.) tail.

Using crochet hook, work 25ch on each side
using the 64 cm (25 in.) tails left at the
beginning and end of your work. This creates
the ties for your cat hat.

ANTLERS
(Make 2)

Using two dpns, cast on 4 sts, leaving a
15 cm (6 in.) tail. Knit a row. Do not
turn needle. Holding one piece of pipe cleaner
in place, slide the 4 sts to other end of needle,
bring yarn around from the back, encasing
the pipe cleaner, and knit the 4 sts again.
This forms the i-cord technique. This
technique, when worked with the pipe cleaner
in the centre, will cover the pipe cleaner and
form a bendable antler. Work in this method
until pipe cleaner is covered, leaving 1 cm
(½ in.) of pipe cleaner exposed at the bottom
for securing antler to the base. To finish, cut
20 cm (8 in.) tail and thread through sts on
needle using a yarn needle.

Weave tail through antler, leaving it at the
base to stitch antler in place.

Next, pick up 2 sts 0.5 cm (¼ in.) from top of
antler and knit 5 rows with i-cord technique.

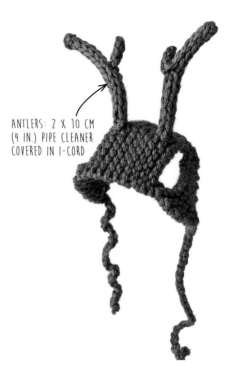

ANTLERS: 2 X 10 CM
(4 IN.) PIPE CLEANER
COVERED IN I-CORD

Weave in ends, pulling them through
antler to base and clipping so that the
ends are not exposed.

ASSEMBLY

With smaller points facing inwards, attach
antlers as follows. Position antler 0.5 cm
(¼ in.) from the ear opening and centre
the antler on the hat. Poke the exposed
pipe cleaner through the base, using a
knitting needle as a guide. Bring the
exposed end back up through the base and
twist it around itself securely. Using a
yarn needle, stitch the base of the antler
to the base of the hat. Stitch so that the
pipe cleaner is no longer exposed and the
antler sits upright. Pull both tails through
to underside of hat, and knot the ends to
anchor the antler.

Repeat with second antler.

JASPER HELPS WITH THE WRAPPING
IN HIS FESTIVE OUTFIT.

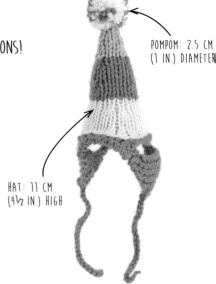

THIS STRIPED HAT IS PURRFECT FOR CAT CELEBRATIONS!

PARTY HAT

POMPOM: 2.5 CM
(1 IN.) DIAMETER

HAT: 11 CM
(4½ IN.) HIGH

BASE
Using yarn A and two dpns, cast on 3 sts, leaving a 64 cm (25 in.) tail.
Row 1: Knit.
Row 2: Kfb, k to last st, kfb. (5 sts)
Rep last 2 rows five more times. (15 sts)
FIRST EAR HOLE
Row 13: K3, cast off next 10 sts, k last st.
Row 14: K2, cast on 10 sts, k3. (The 3 st side is the front of the hat.)
MIDDLE SECTION
Knit 16 rows.
SECOND EAR HOLE
Row 31: K3, cast off next 10 sts, k last st.
Row 32: K2, cast on 10 sts, k3.
Row 33: Knit.
Row 34: K2tog, k to last 2 sts, k2tog. (13 sts)
Rep last 2 rows five more times. (3 sts)
Cast off, leaving a 64 cm (25 in.) tail.

To create ties, using crochet hook and 64 cm (25 in.) tail, pull a loop through each stitch on cast off edge (3 loops), yo, pull one loop through, work 25ch, pull end through loop tightly and snip extra yarn. Repeat with other 64 cm (25 in.) tail.

HAT
Using yarn B, cast on 30 sts, leaving a 50 cm (20 in.) tail. Divide onto three dpns (10 sts per needle) and join to work in the round.
Rnds 1–2: Knit.
Rnd 3: [K2tog, k6, k2tog] 3 times. (24 sts)
Rnds 4–7: Knit.
Rnd 8: [K2tog, k4, k2tog] 3 times. (18 sts)
Rnds 9–10: Knit.
Change to yarn A.

Rnds 11–14: Knit.
Rnd 15: [K2, k2tog, k2] 3 times. (15 sts)
Rnds 16–19: Knit.
Rnd 20: [K1, k2tog, k2] 3 times. (12 sts)
Change to yarn C.
Rnds 21–24: Knit.
Rnd 25: [K1, k2tog, k1] 3 times. (9 sts)
Rnds 26–28: Knit.
Rnd 29: [K2tog] 4 times, k1. (5 sts)
Rnd 30: [K2tog] twice, k1. (3 sts)
Cut yarn and pull through sts on needle.
Pull closed, and weave end into inside of hat.

ASSEMBLY
Make a 2.5 cm (1 in.) pompom using all three yarn colours. Secure to top of hat. Weave ends into the inside of the hat and secure in place. Lightly stuff hat with polyester fibre filling. Do not overfill. Using the cast on tail from the hat, stitch the hat onto the middle section of the base. Stitch into the cast on edge of the hat, until hat is securely in place. Weave end through to underside of base and tie securely.

MOOCH GETS IN THE PARTY MOOD WITH THIS STRIPED POMPOM HAT.

SIZE

TO FIT AN AVERAGE ADULT CAT

- EAR OPENING: 5 CM (2 IN.)
- WIDTH OF HAT BETWEEN EARS: 5 CM (2 IN.)

SUPPLIES

- 23 M (25 YD) ARAN WEIGHT YARN IN A (PINK)
- 9 M (10 YD) ARAN WEIGHT YARN IN B (WHITE)
- 9 M (10 YD) ARAN WEIGHT YARN IN C (MINT)
- 4.5 MM DPNS
- 3.75 MM CROCHET HOOK
- YARN NEEDLE
- POLYESTER FIBRE FILLING
- POMPOM MAKER (OPTIONAL)

SKILL LEVEL: DIFFICULT

SIZE

TO FIT AN AVERAGE
ADULT CAT

- EAR OPENING: 6 CM
(2½ IN.)

- WIDTH OF HAT BETWEEN
EARS: 6 CM (2½ IN.)

✳✳✳✳✳

SUPPLIES

- 37 M (40 YD) ARAN
WEIGHT YARN IN A
(PURPLE)

- 14 M (15 YD) ARAN
WEIGHT YARN IN B
(GREEN)

- 4.5 MM DPNS

- 4 MM CROCHET HOOK

- YARN NEEDLE

- POLYESTER FIBRE FILLING

YOUR CAT WILL BEWITCH AND BEGUILE IN THIS HAT,
ESPECIALLY ON HALLOWEEN! HAVE FUN WITH THE
COLOURS ON THIS PROJECT – USE A SPARKLY YARN
FOR AN ESPECIALLY ENCHANTING LOOK.

WITCH

HAT: 7.5 CM
(3 IN.) HIGH

BASE
Using yarn A and two dpns, cast on
3 sts, leaving a 64 cm (25 in.) tail.
Row 1: Knit.
Row 2: Kfb, k to last st, kfb. (5 sts)
Rep last 2 rows five more times.
(15 sts)
FIRST EAR HOLE
Row 13: K2, cast off next 11 sts, k last st.
Row 14: K2, cast on 11 sts, k2.
MIDDLE SECTION
Knit 16 rows.
SECOND EAR HOLE
Row 31: K2, cast off next 11 sts, k last st.
Row 32: K2, cast on 11 sts, k2.
Row 33: Knit.
Row 34: K2tog, k to last 2 sts, k2tog. (13 sts)
Rep last 2 rows five more times. (3 sts)
Cast off, leaving a 64 cm (25 in.) tail.

To create ties, using crochet hook and 64 cm (25 in.) tail,
pull a loop through each stitch on cast off edge (3 loops),
yo, pull one loop through, work 25ch, pull end through
loop tightly and snip extra yarn. Repeat with other 64 cm
(25 in.) tail.

HAT
Using yarn B, cast on 30 sts, leaving a 38 cm (15 in.) tail.
Distribute sts evenly across three dpns (10 sts per needle)
and join to work in the round.
Rnds 1–3: Knit.
Change to yarn A.
Rnd 4: Knit.

Rnd 5: [K1, k2tog, k4, k2tog, k1] 3 times. (24 sts)
Rnds 6–8: Knit.
Rnd 9: [K1, k2tog, k2, k2tog, k1] 3 times. (18 sts)
Rnds 10–12: Knit.
Rnd 13: [K1, (k2tog) twice, k1] 3 times. (12 sts)
Rnds 14–16: Knit.
Rnd 17: K2tog around. (6 sts)
Rnds 18–20: Knit.
Cut yarn, leaving a 15 cm (6 in.) tail, and pull through
loops on needle. If desired, run a hidden stitch 1 cm
(½ in.) from the top of the hat and tug, to give the hat
a rumpled look. Knot yarn on underside of hat to keep
effect in place.

Using polyester fibre filling, lightly stuff hat. Do not
overfill. Centre the hat on the middle of the base and stitch
into place using yarn B tail. Stitch along cast on edge of
hat. Once finished, secure to underside of hat base.

FALL UNDER THE SPELL OF LINK,
THE ENCHANTING BIRMAN.

AN ODE TO A FAVOURITE TREAT! HAVE FUN WITH
THE TOPPINGS ON YOUR 'CUPCAKE!'

CUPCAKE

CUPCAKE AND
CASE: 7.5 CM
(3 IN.) HIGH

BASE

Using yarn A and two dpns, cast on
3 sts, leaving a 64 cm (25 in.) tail.
Row 1: Knit.
Row 2: Kfb, k to last st, kfb. (5 sts)
Rep last 2 rows five more times. (15 sts)
FIRST EAR HOLE
Row 13: K2, cast off next 11 sts, k last st.
Row 14: K2, cast on 11 sts, k2.
MIDDLE SECTION
Knit 16 rows.
SECOND EAR HOLE
Row 31: K2, cast off next 11 sts, k last st.
Row 32: K2, cast on 11 sts, k2.
Row 33: Knit.
Row 34: K2tog, k to last 2 sts, k2tog.
(13 sts)
Rep last 2 rows five more times. (3 sts)
Cast off, leaving a 64 cm (25 in.) tail.

To create ties, using crochet hook and
64 cm (25 in.) tail, pull a loop through
each stitch on cast off edge (3 loops),
yo, pull one loop through, work 25ch,
pull end through loop tightly and snip
extra yarn. Repeat with other 25 in.
(64 cm) tail.

CUPCAKE CASE

Using yarn B and two dpns, cast on 6 sts.
Knit 30 rows.
Cast off.
Sew ends together.
Weave tails to the bottom of the band.

CUPCAKE

Using yarn C, pick up 30 sts along edge of
band. Place 10 sts on each of three dpns.
Knit 5 rnds.
Rnd 6: [K3, k2tog] to end. (24 sts)
Rnds 7–8: Knit.
Rnd 9: [K2, k2tog] to end. (18 sts)
Rnd 10: Knit.
Rnd 11: [K1, k2tog] to end. (12 sts)
Rnd 12: Knit.
Rnd 13: K2tog around. (6 sts)
Cut yarn and pull through loops
on needles.

SPRINKLES
Using yarn A, thread yarn needle and
sew short stitches on the white 'icing'
in random spots for a sprinkle effect.
Secure yarn to inside of cupcake.

Stuff cupcake with polyester fibre
filling. Stitch cupcake to the base of the
hat, slightly off centre, using the tails
from the cupcake case.

SKILL LEVEL: DIFFICULT

SIZE

TO FIT AN AVERAGE
ADULT CAT

- EAR OPENING: 6 CM
  (2½ IN.)
- WIDTH OF HAT BETWEEN
  EARS: 6 CM (2½ IN.)

SUPPLIES

- 27 M (30 YD) ARAN
  WEIGHT YARN IN A
  (LIGHT PINK)

- 14 M (15 YD) ARAN
  WEIGHT YARN IN B
  (HOT PINK)

- 14 M (15 YD) ARAN
  WEIGHT YARN IN C
  (WHITE)

- 4.5 MM DPNS

- 4 MM CROCHET HOOK

- YARN NEEDLE

- POLYESTER FIBRE FILLING

METHOD: KNIT

SKILL LEVEL: DIFFICULT

SIZE

TO FIT AN AVERAGE
ADULT CAT

- EAR OPENING: 6 CM
  (2½ IN.)
- WIDTH OF HAT BETWEEN
  EARS: 6 CM (2½ IN.)

SUPPLIES

- 37 M (40 YD) CHUNKY
  WEIGHT YARN IN A (YELLOW)
- 2.7 M (3 YD) CHUNKY WEIGHT
  YARN IN B (BROWN)
- 4.5 MM DPNS
- 4 MM CROCHET HOOK
- YARN NEEDLE

WHAT DOES YOUR CAT GO BANANAS FOR? THESE KITTIES ARE
BANANAS FOR BANANA HATS!

BANANA

BANANA: 10 CM
(4 IN.) HIGH

BASE
Using yarn A and two dpns, cast on 3 sts,
leaving a 64 cm (25 in.) tail.
Row 1: Knit.
Row 2: Kfb, k to last st, kfb. (5 sts)
Rep last 2 rows five more times. (15 sts)
FIRST EAR HOLE
Row 13: K2, cast off next 11 sts, k last st.
Row 14: K2, cast on 11 sts, k2.
MIDDLE SECTION
Knit 16 rows.
SECOND EAR HOLE
Row 31: K2, cast off next 11 sts, k last st.
Row 32: K2, cast on 11 sts, k2.
Row 33: Knit.
Row 34: K2tog, k to last 2 sts, k2tog.
(13 sts)
Rep last 2 rows five more times. (3 sts)
Cast off, leaving a 64 cm (25 in.) tail.

To create ties, using crochet hook and 64 cm
(25 in.) tail, pull a loop through each stitch
on cast off edge (3 loops), yo, pull one loop
through, work 25ch, pull end through loop
tightly and snip extra yarn. Repeat with
other 64 cm (25 in.) tail.

BANANA
Using yarn A, cast on 20 sts, leaving a 38 cm
(15 in.) tail. Divide sts evenly onto three
dpns and join to work in the round.

Rnds 1–6: Knit.
Rnd 7: K14, k2tog, k2,
k2tog. (18 sts)
Rnds 8–12: Knit.
Rnd 13: K5, [k2tog] twice,
k9. (16 sts)
Rnd 14: K4, [k2tog] twice,
k6. (14 sts)
Rnd 15: K3, [k2tog] twice,
k7. (12 sts)
Rnds 16–18: Knit.
Rnd 19: K2, [k2tog] twice, k6. (10 sts)
Rnd 20: Knit.
Rnd 21: K1, [k2tog] twice, k1, [k2tog]
twice. (6 sts)
Change to yarn B.
Knit 4 rnds.
Cut yarn and pull through loops on needles.

ASSEMBLY
You should have a 'flat side' to the banana –
that side is the front. Stuff with polyester
fibre filling, being mindful that the front
should lay flat and the rest should curve.
Use the blunt edge of a knitting needle to
help stuff the stem of the banana if necessary.
Attach to the middle of the base, centring
the banana, and making sure the front of
the banana is facing the front of the base
(either side of the base can be the front).
Using cast on tail, securely attach the banana
to the hat base by stitching along the cast on
edge of the banana. When finished, tie off to
underside of base.

GUS GOES TO EXTREME LENGTHS TO
CAMOUFLAGE HIMSELF WHILE ON THE PROWL.

METHOD: KNIT

SKILL LEVEL: DIFFICULT

SIZE

TO FIT AN AVERAGE
ADULT CAT

- EAR OPENING: 5 CM (2 IN.)
- WIDTH OF HAT BETWEEN
  EARS: 5 CM (2 IN.)

SUPPLIES

- 23 M (25 YD) CHUNKY
  WEIGHT YARN IN A (RED)
- 9 M (10 YD) CHUNKY
  WEIGHT YARN IN B
  (WHITE)
- 4.5 MM DPNS
- 4 MM CROCHET HOOK
- YARN NEEDLE
- POMPOM MAKER
  (OPTIONAL)

A CLASSIC SANTA HAT, SLIGHTLY SLOUCHY AND KNITTED IN RICH COLOURS. ITS NOSTALGIC LOOK IS GREAT FOR SEASONAL PHOTOS!

SANTA HAT

BASE

Using yarn A and two dpns, cast on 3 sts, leaving a 64 cm (25 in.) tail.

Row 1: Knit.

Row 2: Kfb, k to last st, kfb. (5 sts)

Rep last 2 rows five more times. (15 sts)

FIRST EAR HOLE

Row 13: K2, cast off next 11 sts, k last st.

Row 14: K2, cast on 11 sts, k2.

MIDDLE SECTION

Knit 16 rows.

SECOND EAR HOLE

Row 31: K2, cast off next 11 sts, k last st.

Row 32: K2, cast on 11 sts, k2.

Row 33: Knit.

Row 34: K2tog, k to last 2 sts, k2tog. (13 sts)

Rep last 2 rows five more times. (3 sts)

Cast off, leaving a 64 cm (25 in.) tail.

To create ties, using crochet hook and 64 cm (25 in.) tail, pull a loop through each stitch on cast off edge (3 loops), yo, pull one loop through, work 25ch, pull end through loop tightly and snip extra yarn. Repeat with other 64 cm (25 in.) tail.

IF YOU'VE BEEN GOOD GIRLS AND BOYS, LINK MAY DELIVER YOUR CHRISTMAS PRESENTS.

HAT

Using yarn A, cast on 30 sts, leaving a 25 in.
(64 cm) tail. Divide sts evenly over three dpns
(10 sts per needle). Being careful not to twist sts,
join to work in the round.

Rnds 1–4: Knit.
Rnd 5: [K2tog, k6, k2tog] 3 times. (24 sts)
Rnds 6–9: Knit.
Rnd 10: [K2tog, k4, k2tog] 3 times. (18 sts)
Rnds 11–12: Knit.
Rnd 13: [K2tog, k2, k2tog] 3 times. (12 sts)
Rnds 14–15: Knit.
Rnd 16: [K2tog] 6 times. (6 sts)
Rnd 17: Knit.
Rnd 18: [K2tog] 3 times. (3 sts)
Cut yarn, leaving a 25 cm (10 in.) tail. Pull
through loops on needle and securely close
top of hat.

To slouch hat, use the cast off tail and weave yarn
through sts until yarn is about 2.5 cm (1 in.) from
top. Tug until desired slouch is achieved. Knot
yarn on inside to secure slouch.

ASSEMBLY

Stitch the hat to the base using the long cast on
tail from the hat. Centre the hat, and stitch evenly
through the cast on edge. The hat should reach the
edge of the front and back of the base.

Make a 2.5 cm (1 in.) pompom with yarn B. Attach
to the top of the hat.

TRIM

Using yarn B and crochet hook, begin on right side
of base and work double crochet evenly along front
edge of base. Weave in ends to the underside of hat
base and secure.

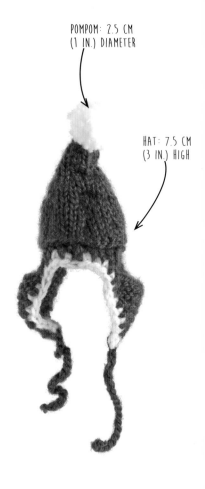

POMPOM: 2.5 CM
(1 IN.) DIAMETER

HAT: 7.5 CM
(3 IN.) HIGH

WHO BETTER TO WISH YOUR
FREINDS AND FAMILY SEASON'S
GREETINGS THAN DAISY?

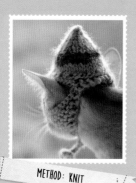

SIZE

TO FIT A SMALL
ADULT CAT

- EAR OPENING: 5 CM (2 IN.)
- WIDTH OF HAT BETWEEN
  EARS: 5 CM (2 IN.)

SUPPLIES

- 37 M (40 YD) CHUNKY
  WEIGHT YARN IN A
  (GREEN)
- 9 M (10 YD) CHUNKY
  WEIGHT YARN IN B (RED)
- 4.5 MM DPNS
- 4 MM CROCHET HOOK
- YARN NEEDLE
- POLYESTER FIBRE FILLING

SANTA'S LITTLE HELPER LOOKS PURRFECT IN THIS FESTIVE HAT!

ELF

BASE

Using yarn A and two dpns, cast on 3 sts, leaving a 64 cm (25 in.) tail.

Row 1: Knit.

Row 2: Kfb, k to last st, kfb. (5 sts)

Rep last 2 rows five more times. (15 sts)

FIRST EAR HOLE

Row 13: K2, cast off next 11 sts, k last st.

Row 14: K2, cast on 11 sts, k2.

MIDDLE SECTION

Knit 16 rows.

SECOND EAR HOLE

Row 31: K2, cast off 11 next sts, k last st.

Row 32: K2, cast on 11 sts, k2.

Row 33: Knit.

Row 34: K2tog, k to last 2 sts, k2tog. (13 sts)

Rep last 2 rows five more times. (3 sts)

Cast off, leaving a 64 cm (25 in.) tail.

To create ties, using crochet hook and 64 cm (25 in.) tail, pull a loop through each stitch on cast off edge (3 loops), yo, pull one loop through, work 25ch, pull end through loop tightly and snip extra yarn. Repeat with other 64 cm (25 in.) tail.

HAT

Using yarn A, cast on 30 sts, leaving a 38 cm (15 in.) tail. Divide sts evenly onto three dpns (10 sts per needle). Join to begin working in the round.

Rnds 1–3: Knit.

Change to yarn B.

Rnd 4: Knit.

Rnd 5: [K3, k2tog] around. (24 sts)

Rnd 6: Knit.

Change to yarn A.

Rnd 7: [K2, k2tog] around. (18 sts)

Rnd 8: Knit.

Rnd 9: [K1, k2tog] around. (12 sts)

Rnds 10–11: Knit.

Rnd 12: K2tog around. (6 sts)

Rnd 13: Knit.

Rnd 14: K2tog around. (3 sts)

Cut yarn and pull through loops. Lightly stuff hat with polyester fibre filling. Stitch to middle section of base using cast on tail from hat.

VIVI IS COUNTING DOWN THE DAYS UNTIL CHRISTMAS!

MOOCH IS READY TO
RAZZLE DAZZLE IN
HIS TOP HAT.

A CLASSIC TOP HAT FOR FANCY FELINES EVERYWHERE!
A BIT OF SPARKLE MAKES THIS SUITABLE FOR SPECIAL
OCCASIONS OR RINGING IN A NEW YEAR!

TOP HAT

METHOD: KNIT

SKILL LEVEL: DIFFICULT

BASE

Using yarn A and two dpns, cast on 3 sts, leaving
a 51 cm (20 in.) tail.
Row 1: Knit.
Row 2: Kfb, k to last st, kfb. (5 sts)
Rep last 2 rows three more times. (11 sts)
FIRST EAR HOLE
Row 9: K1, cast off next 9 sts.
Row 10: K1, cast on 9 sts, k1.
MIDDLE SECTION
Knit 16 rows.
SECOND EAR HOLE
Row 27: K1, cast off next 9 sts.
Row 28: K1, cast on 9 sts, k1.
Row 29: Knit.
Row 30: K2tog, k to last 2 sts, k2tog. (9 sts)
Rep last 2 rows three more times. (3 sts)
Cast off, leaving a 51 cm (20 in.) tail.

To create ties, using crochet hook and 51 cm (20 in.)
tail, pull a loop through each stitch on cast off edge
(3 loops), yo, pull one loop through, work 25ch, pull
end through loop tightly and snip extra yarn. Repeat
with other 51 cm (20 in.) tail.

TOP HAT
TOP OF HAT
To get a flat top for the hat, you will be creating
a flap that will need to be stitched into place later,
so that the hat has a smooth top.
Using yarn B and two dpns, cast on 1 st, leaving
a 10 cm (4 in.) tail.

SIZE

TO FIT AN AVERAGE ADULT CAT
- EAR OPENING: 5 CM (2 IN.)
- WIDTH OF HAT BETWEEN EARS:
  6 CM (2½ IN.)

✳ ✳ ✳ ✳ ✳

SUPPLIES

- 14 M (15 YD) ARAN WEIGHT YARN
  IN A (BLACK)
- 41 M (45 YD) SPARKLY 4-PLY YARN
  IN B (BROWN)
- 4.5 MM DPNS
- POLYESTER FIBRE FILLING
- YARN NEEDLE
- 4.5 MM CROCHET HOOK
- 1 CM (½ IN.) WIDE BLACK SATIN
  RIBBON (OPTIONAL)

Row 1: [K1, p1, k1] all into st. (3 sts)
Row 2: Purl.
Row 3: Kfb of all sts. (6 sts)
Row 4: Purl.
Row 3: Kfb of all sts. (12 sts)
Divide sts onto three dpns (4 sts per needle) and join to work in the round.
Next rnd: Knit.
Next rnd: [Kfb, k1] around. (18 sts)
Next rnd: Knit.
Next rnd: [Kfb, k2] around. (24 sts)
Next rnd: Knit.
Next rnd: [Kfb, k3] around. (30 sts)
Next rnd: Purl.

TUBE OF HAT
Knit 15 rnds.
Cast off, leaving a 51 cm (20 in.) tail. Using the cast on tail, stitch the flap created on the top of the hat into place, so that it lies flat. Next, using the 51 cm (20 in.) tail, begin stitching the top hat in place on the base of the cat hat. Centre the top hat on the middle section of the base, stitching into the cast off edge of the top hat. Once you have stitched halfway around the hat, lightly stuff the hat with polyester fibre filling. Overstuffing will give the wrong shape. Continue stitching around the cast off edge of the hat until it is securely in place. Weave in ends of hat securely on underside of the base and snip.

BRIM
Using yarn B and two dpns, cast on 6 sts, leaving a 10 cm (4 in.) tail. Knit every row until band measures 23 cm (9 in.). Cast off, leaving a 51 cm (20 in.) tail. Stitch ends of the brim together using cast on tail. Weave in tail and snip. Slide the brim over the top hat, to the bottom of the top hat. Using the 51 cm (20 in.) tail, stitch the brim onto the base of the hat, following along the cast off edge of the top hat. When finished, pull end through the underside of the cat hat base, weave in securely and snip.

Once stitched into place, use a length of yarn B and a yarn needle to create some simple stitches that will anchor the brim into the

appropriate shape. The brim will naturally roll, though you want the front to be flat. You can place a few small stitches on each side of the front brim, to secure the roll and keep the front flat. Weave in any ends to underside of the base and snip.

Measure ribbon around the bottom of the hat, add 2.5 cm (1 in.) and cut. Fold one end over 1 cm (½ in.), then fold over 1 cm (½ in.) again. Using matching thread and a needle, stitch this fold into place. Wrap the ribbon around the bottom of hat, secure raw end under the fold and stitch in place to create the band.

HAT: 5 CM (2 IN.) DIAMETER

HAT: 5 CM (2 IN.) HIGH

RIBBON: 1 CM (½ IN.) WIDE

SIZE

TO FIT A SMALL
ADULT CAT

- EAR OPENING: 5 CM (2 IN.)
- WIDTH OF HAT BETWEEN
EARS: 5 CM (2 IN.)

✳ ✳ ✳ ✳ ✳

SUPPLIES

- 18 M (20 YD) ARAN
WEIGHT YARN IN A (PINK)
- 4.5 M (5 YD) ARAN
WEIGHT YARN IN B
(GREEN)
- 5 MM CROCHET HOOK
- YARN NEEDLE
- POMPOM MAKER
(OPTIONAL)

THIS PEPPY POMPOM HAT IS THE PERFECT ACCESSORY
FOR ANY HIGH-SPIRITED KITTY.

POMPOM HAT

BASE

Using yarn A, work 2ch, leaving a
64 cm (25 in.) tail.
Row 1: 3dc in 2nd ch, 1ch.
Row 2: 3dc, 1ch.
Row 3: 2dc in first st, 1dc, 2dc in
last st, 1ch. (5dc)
Row 4: 5dc, 1ch.
Row 5: 2dc in first st, 3dc, 2dc in
last st, 1ch. (7dc)
Row 6: 7dc, 1ch.
Row 7: 2dc in first st, 5dc, 2dc in
last st, 1ch. (9dc)
Row 8: 9dc, 1ch.
Row 9: 2dc in first st, 7dc, 2dc in
last st, 1ch. (11dc)
FIRST EAR HOLE
Row 10: 1dc, 9ch, 1dc in last st, 1ch.
MIDDLE SECTION
Rows 11–20: 11dc, 1ch.
SECOND EAR HOLE
Row 21: 1dc, 9ch, 1dc in last st, 1ch.
Row 22: 11dc, 1ch.
Row 23: 1dc, skip next st, 7dc, skip
next st, 1dc, 1ch. (9dc)
Row 24: 9dc, 1ch.
Row 25: 1dc, skip next st, 5dc, skip
next st, 1dc, 1ch. (7dc)
Row 26: 7dc, 1ch.
Row 27: 1dc, skip next st, 3dc, skip
next st, 1dc, 1ch. (5dc)
Row 28: 5dc, 1ch.
Row 29: 1dc, skip next st, 1dc, skip
next st, 1dc, 1ch. (3dc)
Row 30: 3dc, 1ch.
Row 31: 1dc in last st.

BASE

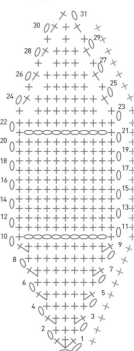

○ ch
+ dc

RACHEL IS PROUD TO WEAR HER COLOURFUL, FLUFFY POMPOM CAP.

To create ties, work 25ch, snip yarn and pull through loop. Trim tail. Work 25ch at the beg of base, using 64 cm (25 in.) tail.

FRONT TRIM
Holding yarns A and B together, work 30dc across front of hat base. Clip yarn, pull through loop and fasten securely on underside of the hat.

Make a 2.5 cm (1 in.) pompom from yarns A and B and attach to centre of hat.

This is an easy design to adapt. Use your favourite sports team colours or holiday colours to make it your own.

POMPOM:
2.5 CM (1 IN.)
DIAMETER

SIZE

TO FIT AN AVERAGE
ADULT CAT
- EAR OPENING: 6 CM
  (2½ IN.)
- WIDTH OF HAT BETWEEN
  EARS: 6 CM (2½ IN.)

SUPPLIES

- 27 M (30 YD) ARAN
  WEIGHT YARN IN A
  (LIGHT ORANGE)
- 27 M (30 YD) ARAN
  WEIGHT YARN IN B
  (DARK ORANGE)
- 4 MM CROCHET HOOK
- 3.5 MM CROCHET HOOK
- YARN NEEDLE

FOR THE LITTLE LION WHO THINKS HE'S A BIG ONE!

LITTLE LION

BASE

Using yarn A and 4 mm
hook, work 2ch, leaving a
64 cm (25 in.) tail.
Row 1: 3dc in 2nd ch, 1ch.
Row 2: 3dc, 1ch.
Row 3: 2dc in first st, 1dc, 2dc
in last st, 1ch. (5dc)
Row 4: 5dc, 1ch.
Row 5: 2dc in first st, 3dc, 2dc
in last st, 1ch. (7dc)
Row 6: 7dc, 1ch.
Row 7: 2dc in first st, 5dc, 2dc
in last st, 1ch. (9dc)
Row 8: 9dc, 1ch.
Row 9: 2dc in first st, 7dc, 2dc
in last st, 1ch. (11dc)
Row 10: 11dc, 1ch.
Row 11: 2dc in first st, 9dc, 2dc
in last st, 1ch. (13dc)
Row 12: 13dc, 1ch.
Row 13: 2dc in first st, 11dc,
2dc in last st, 1ch. (15dc)
FIRST EAR HOLE
Row 14: 1dc, 13ch, 1dc in last
st, 1ch.
MIDDLE SECTION
Rows 15–26: 15dc, 1ch.
SECOND EAR HOLE
Row 27: 1dc, 13ch, 1dc in last
st, 1ch.
Row 28: 15dc, 1ch.
Row 29: 1dc, skip next st, 11dc,
skip next st, 1dc, 1ch. (13dc)
Row 30: 13dc, 1ch.
Row 31: 1dc, skip next st, 9dc,
skip next st, 1dc, 1ch. (11dc)

MANE: 2 ROWS
OF 40 LOOPS

Row 32: 11dc, 1ch.

Row 33: 1dc, skip next st, 7dc, skip next st, 1dc, 1ch. (9dc)

Row 34: 9dc, 1ch.

Row 35: 1dc, skip next st, 5dc, skip next st, 1dc, 1ch. (7dc)

Row 36: 7dc, 1ch.

Row 37: 1dc, skip next st, 3dc, skip next st, 1dc, 1ch. (5dc)

Row 38: 5dc, 1ch.

Row 39: 1dc, skip next st, 1dc, skip next st, 1dc, 1ch. (3dc)

Row 40: 1dc in last st. Work 25ch, snip yarn and pull through loop tightly. Trim tail. Work 25ch at beg of base, using 64 cm (25 in.) tail.

MANE

Using yarn B and 3.5 mm hook, work the mane evenly along the front edge of the hat base.

Starting just above the right tie:

Row 1: [Sl st in next sp, 8ch, sl st in same sp] rep across hat, making 40 loops.

Turn work. You will now work on top of the hat base, creating a second row of slightly larger loops.

Row 2: [Sl st in next sp, 12ch, sl st in same sp] rep across hat, making 40 loops and ending on the side the mane started on.

ASSEMBLY

Pull all ends to underside of hat and secure in place.

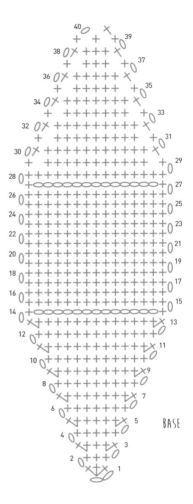

BASE

MANE ROW 1

MANE ROW 2

○ ch
● sl st
+ dc

WATCH OUT! POPPY IS ON THE PROWL.

METHOD: CROCHET

SKILL LEVEL: INTERMEDIATE

SIZE

TO FIT AN AVERAGE
ADULT CAT

- EAR OPENING: 5 CM (2 IN.)
- WIDTH OF HAT BETWEEN
  EARS: 6 CM (2½ IN.)

SUPPLIES

- 27 M (30 YD) ARAN
  WEIGHT YARN IN A
  (ORANGE)
- 9 M (10 YD) ARAN WEIGHT
  YARN IN B (WHITE)
- 2.7 M (3 YD) CHUNKY
  WEIGHT YARN IN C
  (BLACK)
- 4 MM CROCHET HOOK
- 3.5 MM CROCHET HOOK
- YARN NEEDLE

A CRAFTY HAT FOR YOUR CUNNING CAT!
CHICKENS BEWARE!

FELINE FOX

BASE

Using yarn A and 4 mm hook, work 2ch, leaving a
64 cm (25 in.) tail.
Row 1: 3dc in 2nd ch, 1ch.
Row 2: 3dc, 1ch.
Row 3: 2dc in first st, 1dc, 2dc in last st, 1ch. (5dc)
Row 4: 5dc, 1ch.
Row 5: 2dc in first st, 3dc, 2dc in last st, 1ch. (7dc)
Row 6: 7dc, 1ch.
Row 7: 2dc in first st, 5dc, 2dc in last st, 1ch. (9dc)
Row 8: 9dc, 1ch.
Row 9: 2dc in first st, 7dc, 2dc in last st, 1ch. (11dc)
Row 10: 11dc, 1ch.
Row 11: 2dc in first st, 9dc, 2dc in last st, 1ch. (13dc)

FIRST EAR HOLE

Row 12: 1dc, 11ch, 1dc in last st, 1ch.

MIDDLE SECTION

Rows 13–15: 13dc, 1ch.
Row 16: 2dc in first st, dc to end, 1ch. (14dc)
(The increase side is the front of the hat.)
Row 17: 13dc, 2dc in last st, 1ch. (15dc)
Row 18: 2dc in first st, dc to end, 1ch. (16dc)
Row 19: 15dc, 2dc in last st, 1ch. (17dc)
Row 20: Skip first st, 16dc, 1ch. (16dc)
Row 21: 14dc, skip next st, 1dc in last st,
1ch. (15dc)
Row 22: Skip first st, 14dc, 1ch. (14dc)
Row 23: 12dc, skip next st, 1dc in last st,
1ch. (13dc)
Rows 24–26: 13dc, 1ch.

DOMINO HAS A FANTASTIC
FOXY MAKEOVER.

SECOND EAR HOLE

Row 27: 1dc, 11ch, 1dc in last st, 1ch.

Row 28: 13dc, 1ch.

Row 29: 1dc, skip next st, 9dc, skip next st, 1dc, 1ch. (11dc)

Row 30: 11dc, 1ch.

Row 31: 1dc, skip next st, 7dc, skip next st, 1dc, 1ch. (9dc)

Row 32: 9dc, 1ch.

Row 33: 1dc, skip next st, 5dc, skip next st, 1dc, 1ch. (7dc)

Row 34: 7dc, 1ch.

Row 35: 1dc, skip next st, 3dc, skip next st, 1dc, 1ch. (5dc)

Row 36: 5dc, 1ch.

Row 37: 1dc, skip next st, 1dc, skip next st, 1dc, 1ch. (3dc)

Row 38: 3dc, 1ch.

Row 39: 1dc in last st.

To create ties, work 25ch, snip yarn and pull through loop tightly. Trim tail. Work 25ch at beg of base, using 64 cm (25 in.) tail.

OUTER EARS
(Make 2)

Using yarn A and 3.5 mm hook, work 3ch.

Row 1: Skip first ch, 2dc, 1ch.

Row 2: 2dc, 1ch.

Row 3: 2dc in each st, 1ch. (4dc)

Row 4: 4dc, 1ch.

Row 5: 2dc in first st, 2dc, 2dc in last st, 1ch. (6dc)

Row 6: 6dc, 1ch.

Row 7: 2dc in first st, 4dc, 2dc in last st, 1ch. (8dc)

Row 8: 8dc, 1ch.

Row 9: 2dc in first st, 6dc, 2dc in last st, 1ch. (10dc)

Rows 10–11: 10dc, 1ch.

Cut a 25 cm (10 in.) tail and pull through loop.

Weave in other tail at point of ear.

INNER EARS
(Make 2)

Using yarn B and 3.5 mm hook, work 3ch.

Row 1: Skip first ch, 2dc, 1ch.

Row 2: 2dc, 1ch.

Row 3: 2dc in each st, 1ch. (4dc)

Row 4: 4dc, 1ch.

Row 5: 2dc in first st, 2dc, 2dc in last st, 1ch. (6dc)

Rows 6–7: 6dc, 1ch.

Cut yarn, leaving a 25 cm (10 in.) tail, and pull through loop. Weave in other tail at point of ear.

Using yarn C and 3.5 mm hook, work 5 sl sts along upper tip and point of inner ear. Weave in ends to WS of ear and clip.

Attach one inner ear to one outer ear using the inner ear 25 cm (10 in.) tail and a yarn needle. Stitch into place, with the base of the ears (the last rows) matching up. Use the photos for reference if necessary. Be careful not to stitch right through the outer ear as you do not want your stitches to be visible. You can create an invisible stitch by running your needle through the edge of the inner ear and barely through the surface of the outer ear.

ASSEMBLY

Stitch each ear along the front edge of the hat base, in front of each ear hole. The front edge of the base is the pointed edge. Use the yarn tails from the outer ears to stitch into place, running your needle through the edge of the outer ear. The ears are meant to stand up, so you may have to reinforce your stitches to give the ears support.

Stand back and admire your cat's new look!

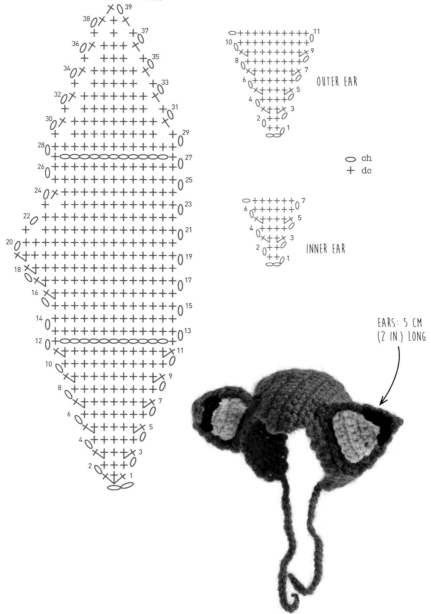

BASE

OUTER EAR

INNER EAR

○ ch
+ dc

EARS: 5 CM
(2 IN.) LONG

SIZE

TO FIT A SMALL ADULT CAT

• EAR OPENING: 5 CM (2 IN.)

• WIDTH OF HAT BETWEEN
  EARS: 5 CM (2 IN.)

SUPPLIES

• 23 M (25 YD) ARAN
  WEIGHT YARN IN A (BROWN)

• 9 M (10 YD) ARAN WEIGHT
  YARN IN B (WHITE)

• 4 MM CROCHET HOOK

• YARN NEEDLE

TRANSFORM YOUR KITTY INTO A CUDDLY TEDDY WITH THIS ADORABLE BEAR HAT.

BABY BEAR

BASE
Using yarn A, work 2ch, leaving a 64 cm (25 in.) tail.

Row 1: 3dc in 2nd ch, 1ch.

Row 2: 3dc, 1ch.

Row 3: 2dc in first st, 1dc, 2dc in last st, 1ch. (5dc)

Row 4: 5dc, 1ch.

Row 5: 2dc in first st, 3dc, 2dc in last st, 1ch. (7dc)

Row 6: 7dc, 1ch.

Row 7: 2dc in first st, 5dc, 2dc in last st, 1ch. (9dc)

Row 8: 9dc, 1ch.

Row 9: 2dc in first st, 7dc, 2dc in last st, 1ch. (11dc)

Row 10: 11dc, 1ch.

Row 11: 2dc in first st, 9dc, 2dc in last st, 1ch. (13dc)

FIRST EAR HOLE
Row 12: 1dc, 11ch, 1dc in last st, 1ch.

MIDDLE SECTION
Rows 13–22: 13dc, 1ch.

SECOND EAR HOLE
Row 23: 1dc, 11ch, 1dc in last st, 1ch.

Row 24: 13dc, 1ch.

Row 25: 1dc, skip next st, 9dc, skip next st, 1dc, 1ch. (11dc)

Row 26: 11dc, 1ch.

Row 27: 1dc, skip next st, 7dc, skip next st, 1dc, 1ch. (9dc)

Row 28: 9dc, 1ch.

EARS: 2.5 X 4 CM
(1 X 1½ IN.)

Row 29: 1dc, skip next st, 5dc, skip next st, 1dc, 1ch. (7dc)
Row 30: 7dc, 1ch.
Row 31: 1dc, skip next st, 3dc, skip next st, 1dc, 1ch. (5dc)
Row 32: 5dc, 1ch.
Row 33: 1dc, skip next st, 1dc, skip next st, 1dc, 1ch. (3dc)
Row 34: 3dc, 1ch.
Row 35: 1dc in last st.

To create ties, work 25ch, snip yarn and pull through loop tightly. Trim tail. Work 25ch at beg of base, using 64 cm (25 in.) tail.

OUTER EARS
(Make 2)
Using yarn A, work 2ch.
Row 1: 2dc in 2nd ch.
Row 2: 2dc in each st. (4dc)
Row 3: 2dc in each st. (8dc)
Row 4: 2dc, 2dc in next 4 sts, 2dc. (12dc)
Row 5: 4dc, 2dc in next 4 sts, 4dc. (16dc)
Cut a 25 cm (10 in.) tail and pull through loop.

INNER EARS
(Make 2)
Using yarn B, work 2ch.
Row 1: 2dc in 2nd ch.
Row 2: 2dc in each st. (4dc)
Row 3: 1dc, 2dc in next 2 sts, 1dc in last st. (6dc)
Cut a 25 cm (10 in.) tail and pull through loop.
Attach to outer ear, lining up the bottom edge of the inner ear to the bottom edge of the outer ear. Be careful as you stitch around inner ear not to stitch all the way through the outer ear, as you don't want the yarn B stitches visible on the back of the outer ear. Repeat with other ear.

ASSEMBLY
Attach the ears along the front edge of the hat base, centred in front of each ear hole. Use the tail from the outer ear to stitch the ears into place. You may need to reinforce your stitches, as the ears are meant to stand up.

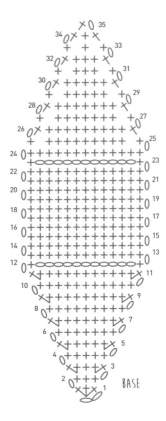

BASE

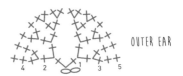

OUTER EAR

INNER EAR

○ ch
+ dc

SIZE

TO FIT AN AVERAGE
ADULT CAT

- EAR OPENING: 5 CM (2 IN.)
- WIDTH OF HAT BETWEEN
  EARS: 5 CM (2 IN.)

SUPPLIES

- 37 M (40 YD) ARAN
  WEIGHT YARN IN A
  (WHITE)
- 18 M (20 YD) ARAN
  WEIGHT YARN IN B
  (BROWN)
- 4 MM CROCHET HOOK
- YARN NEEDLE

THE PERFECT PROJECT FOR DOG- AND CAT-LOVERS!
CUSTOMIZE THE SPOTS, EARS AND COLOURS FOR
DIFFERENT PUPS.

EARS: 5 CM (2 IN.) LONG

DOG

BASE
Using yarn A, work
2ch, leaving a 64 cm
(25 in.) tail.
Row 1: 3dc in 2nd ch, 1ch.
Row 2: 3dc, 1ch.
Row 3: 2dc in first st, 1dc, 2dc in last
st, 1ch. (5dc)
Row 4: 5dc, 1ch.
Row 5: 2dc in first st, 3dc, 2dc in last
st, 1ch. (7dc)
Row 6: 7dc, 1ch.
Row 7: 2dc in first st, 5dc, 2dc in last
st, 1ch. (9dc)
Row 8: 9dc, 1ch.
Row 9: 2dc in first st, 7dc, 2dc in last
st, 1ch. (11dc)
Row 10: 11dc, 1ch.
Row 11: 2dc in first st, 9dc, 2dc in
last st, 1ch. (13dc)
Row 12: 13dc, 1ch.
Row 13: 2dc in first st, 11dc, 2dc in
last st, 1ch. (15dc)
FIRST EAR HOLE
Row 14: 1dc, 13ch, 1dc in last st, 1ch.
MIDDLE SECTION
Rows 15–26: 15dc, 1ch.
SECOND EAR HOLE
Row 27: 1dc, 13ch, 1dc in last st, 1ch.
Row 28: 15dc, 1ch.
Row 29: 1dc, skip next st, 11dc, skip
next st, 1dc, 1ch. (13dc)
Row 30: 13dc, 1ch.

WHO SAYS CATS AND
DOGS CAN'T GET ALONG?
NOT DOMINO!

Row 31: 1dc, skip next st, 9dc, skip next st, 1dc, 1ch. (11dc)
Row 32: 11dc, 1ch.
Row 33: 1dc, skip next st, 7dc, skip next st, 1dc, 1ch. (9dc)
Row 34: 9dc, 1ch.
Row 35: 1dc, skip next st, 5dc, skip next st, 1dc, 1ch. (7dc)
Row 36: 7dc, 1ch.
Row 37: 1dc, skip next st, 3dc, skip next st, 1dc, 1ch. (5dc)
Row 38: 5dc, 1ch.
Row 39: 1dc, skip next st, 1dc, skip next st, 1dc, 1ch. (3dc)
Row 40: 1dc in last st.

To create ties, work 25ch, snip yarn and pull through loop tightly. Trim tail. Work 25ch at beg of base, using 64 cm (25 in.) tail.

EARS
(Make 2)
Using yarn B, make a magic ring.
Rnd 1: 1ch, 10dc in ring.
Rnd 2: 10dc, 1ch.
Rnd 3: [1dc, 2dc in next st] 5 times, 1ch. (15dc)
Rnd 4: 15dc, 1ch.
Rnd 5: Working in back loops only, work 8dc, 1ch, turn.
Continue in rows:
Rows 6–11: 8dc, 1ch.
Cut a 25 cm (10 in.) tail and pull through loop. Weave in beg tail.

SPOTS
(Make 1 in A, 1 in B)
Work 6ch.
Rnd 1: 1dc in 2nd ch, 1dc in next 2ch, 2dc in next ch. Continuing along other side of chain, work 1dc in back loop of next 4ch, sl st to beg dc, 1ch.
Rnd 2: [1dc, 2dc in next st] 3 times, 2dc, 2dc in next st, sl st to beg dc (13dc). Cut a 15 cm (6 in.) tail and pull through loop. Weave in beg tail.

ASSEMBLY
To attach ears, use 25 cm (10 in.) tail to stitch flat side of ear evenly above ear opening on base of hat. Once securely stitched in place, pull tail through to underside of hat and secure. Repeat with other tail.

To attach spots, attach spot in yarn A to one ear. Stitch around spot securely and pull end through to WS of ear. Secure. Attach spot in yarn B to base of hat, underneath the other ear.

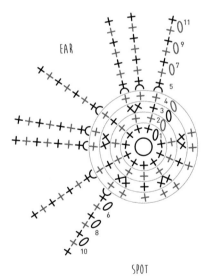

EAR

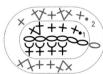

SPOT

⬭	ch
•	sl st
+	dc
⅄	dc in back loops only

BASE

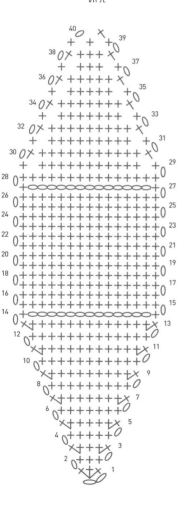

ANNA NICOLE GIVES JAWS A RUN FOR HIS MONEY
IN HER SHARK ATTACK HAT.

LITTLE FISH, BEWARE! SHOWCASE YOUR CAT'S PREDATOR SIDE IN THIS SHARKY HAT!

SHARK ATTACK

BASE
Using yarn A and 5 mm hook, work 2ch, leaving a 64 cm (25 in.) tail.
Row 1: 3dc in 2nd ch, 1ch.
Row 2: 3dc, 1ch.
Row 3: 2dc in first st, 1dc, 2dc in last st, 1ch. (5dc)
Row 4: 5dc, 1ch.
Row 5: 2dc in first st, 3dc, 2dc in last st, 1ch. (7dc)
Row 6: 7dc, 1ch.
Row 7: 2dc in first st, 5dc, 2dc in last st, 1ch. (9dc)
Row 8: 9dc, 1ch.
Row 9: 2dc in first st, 7dc, 2dc in last st, 1ch. (11dc)
Row 10: 11dc, 1ch.
Row 11: 2dc in first st, 9dc, 2dc in last st, 1ch. (13dc)

FIRST EAR HOLE
Row 12: 1dc, 11ch, 1dc in last st, 1ch.

MIDDLE SECTION
Rows 13–22: 13dc, 1ch.

SECOND EAR HOLE
Row 23: 1dc, 11ch, 1dc in last st, 1ch.
Row 24: 13dc, 1ch.
Row 25: 1dc, skip next st, 9dc, skip next st, 1dc, 1ch. (11dc)
Row 26: 11dc, 1ch.
Row 27: 1dc, skip next st, 7dc, skip next st, 1dc, 1ch. (9dc)
Row 28: 9dc, 1ch.
Row 29: 1dc, skip next st, 5dc, skip next st, 1dc, 1ch. (7dc)
Row 30: 7dc, 1ch.

FIN: 6 X 5 CM (2½ X 2 IN.) HIGH

SIZE
TO FIT AN AVERAGE ADULT CAT
- EAR OPENING: 5 CM (2 IN.)
- WIDTH OF HAT BETWEEN EARS: 5 CM (2 IN.)

✳ ✳ ✳ ✳ ✳

SUPPLIES
- 16 M (18 YD) ARAN WEIGHT YARN IN A (BLUE)
- 2.7 M (3 YD) ARAN WEIGHT YARN IN B (RED)
- 4.5 M (5 YD) ARAN WEIGHT YARN IN C (WHITE)
- 5 MM CROCHET HOOK
- 4 MM CROCHET HOOK
- YARN NEEDLE

Row 31: 1dc, skip next st, 3dc, skip next st, 1dc, 1ch. (5dc)
Row 32: 5dc, 1ch.
Row 33: 1dc, skip next st, 1dc, skip next st, 1dc, 1ch. (3dc)
Row 34: 3dc, 1ch.
Row 35: 1dc in last st.

To create ties, work 25ch, snip yarn and pull through loop tightly. Trim tail. Work 25ch at beg of base, using 64 cm (25 in.) tail.

FIN

Using yarn A and 4 mm hook, work 12ch.
Row 1: Skip first ch, 11dc, 1ch.
Row 2: Skip first st, 9dc, 1ch.
Row 3: 7dc, skip next st, 1dc in last st, 1ch. (8dc)
Row 4: 7dc, 1ch. (7dc)
Row 5: 1dc, skip next st, 3dc, skip next st, 1dc, 1ch. (5dc)
Row 6: 1dc, skip next st, 1dc, skip next st, 1dc, 1ch. (3dc)
Row 7: Skip first st, 2dc, 1ch.
Row 8: 2dc, 1ch.
Row 9: Skip first st, 1dc, 1ch.
Row 10: 1dc.
Cut yarn, leaving a 20 cm (8 in.) tail. Weave the tail from the first row through to the last row of the fin. Stitch to the centre of the middle section of the hat base, running needle through the bottom edge of the fin. The fin will be straighter on one side – that's the side that should face the front. Use the pictures for reference if necessary. You may need to reinforce your stitches, as you want the fin to stand upright.

TEETH EDGE

Using yarn B and 4 mm hook, work 34 sl sts evenly along front edge of the hat base. Cut yarn, pull through loop securely and weave in both ends to the underside of the hat.
Next, using yarn C and 4 mm hook, work 4ch through the first red sl st. Slip st in the same sp, 1dc in next red sl st, [4ch and slip st in same sp, 1dc] rep to end of row. Cut yarn, pull through loop securely and weave in both ends to the underside of the hat.

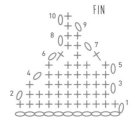

FIN

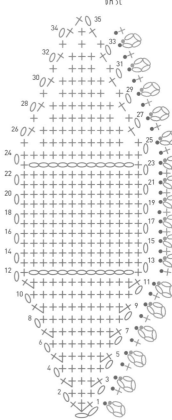

BASE

○ ch
● sl st
+ dc

 METHOD: CROCHET

SKILL LEVEL: DIFFICULT

SIZE

TO FIT AN AVERAGE
ADULT CAT

- EAR OPENING: 5 CM (2 IN.)
- WIDTH OF HAT BETWEEN
  EARS: 6 CM (2½ IN.)

✳ ✳ ✳ ✳ ✳

SUPPLIES

- 27 M (30 YD) ARAN
  WEIGHT YARN IN A (RED)
- 9 M (10 YD) ARAN
  WEIGHT YARN IN B
  (WHITE)
- 4 MM CROCHET HOOK
- YARN NEEDLE
- POLYESTER FIBRE FILLING
- POMPOM MAKER
  (OPTIONAL)

PADDING AROUND ON THE ROOFTOPS, WHO DOES KITTY
DISCOVER? GOOD OLD SANTA CLAUS!

SANTA PAWS

BASE
Using yarn A, work 2ch, leaving a 64 cm
(25 in.) tail.
Row 1: 3dc in 2nd ch, 1ch.
Row 2: 3dc, 1ch.
Row 3: 2dc in first st, 1dc, 2dc in last st,
1ch. (5dc)
Row 4: 5dc, 1ch.
Row 5: 2dc in first st, 3dc, 2dc in last st,
1ch. (7dc)
Row 6: 7dc, 1ch.
Row 7: 2dc in first st, 5dc, 2dc in last st,
1ch. (9dc)
Row 8: 9dc, 1ch.
Row 9: 2dc in first st, 7dc, 2dc in last st,
1ch. (11dc)
Row 10: 11dc, 1ch.
Row 11: 2dc in first st, 9dc, 2dc in last st,
1ch. (13dc)
FIRST EAR HOLE
Row 12: 1dc, 11ch, 1dc in last st, 1ch.
MIDDLE SECTION
Rows 13–22: 13dc, 1ch.
SECOND EAR HOLE
Row 23: 1dc, 11ch, 1dc in last st, 1ch.
Row 24: 13dc, 1ch.
Row 25: 1dc, skip next st, 9dc, skip next st,
1dc, 1ch. (11dc)
Row 26: 11dc, 1ch.
Row 27: 1dc, skip next st, 7dc, skip next st,
1dc, 1ch. (9dc)
Row 28: 9dc, 1ch.

POPPY IS FULL OF FESTIVE
CHEER IN HER SANTA HAT.

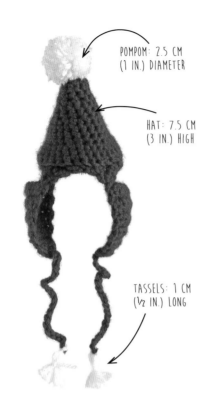

POMPOM: 2.5 CM
(1 IN.) DIAMETER

HAT: 7.5 CM
(3 IN.) HIGH

TASSELS: 1 CM
(½ IN.) LONG

Row 29: 1dc, skip next st, 5dc, skip next st, 1dc, 1ch. (7dc)
Row 30: 7dc, 1ch.
Row 31: 1dc, skip next st, 3dc, skip next st, 1dc, 1ch. (5dc)
Row 32: 5dc, 1ch.
Row 33: 1dc, skip next st, 1dc, skip next st, 1dc, 1ch. (3dc)
Row 34: 3dc, 1ch.
Row 35: 1dc in last st.
Work 25ch, snip yarn and pull through loop tightly. Trim tail. Work 25ch at beg of base, using 64 cm (25 in.) tail.

HAT

Do not join at end of rounds. If necessary, place a marker to show start of round.
Using yarn A, work 2ch.
Rnd 1: 4dc in 2nd ch.
Rnd 2: 1dc in each st around. (4dc)
Rnd 3: 2dc in each st around. (8dc)
Rnds 4–5: 1dc in each st around.
Rnd 6: [1dc, 2dc in next st] 4 times. (12dc)
Rnds 7–9: 1dc in each st around.
Rnd 10: [1dc, 2dc in next st] 6 times. (18dc)
Rnds 11–13: 1dc in each st around.
Rnd 14: [1dc, 2dc in next st] 9 times. (27dc)
Rnds 15–17: 1dc in each st around.
Rnd 18: [2dc, 2dc in next st] 9 times. (36dc)
Rnd 19: [8dc, 2dc in next st] 4 times. (40dc)
Rnds 20–21: 1dc in each st around.

Snip yarn, leaving a 51 cm (20 in.) tail, and pull through loop tightly. Use this tail to attach the hat to the base.

ASSEMBLY

Using yarn B, make a 2.5 cm (1 in.) pompom and two 1 cm (½ in.) tassels. Attach pompom securely to top of hat. Attach one tassel on end of each tie.
Lightly stuff hat top with polyester fibre filling, being careful to evenly distribute filling. Stitch onto centre of the base of hat with 51 cm (20 in.) tail.

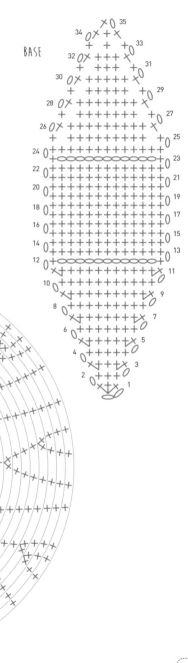

HAT

BASE

○ ch
+ dc

A TRAFFIC-STOPPING HAT PURRFECT FOR THE CATWALK.

TRAFFIC CONE

METHOD: CROCHET

SKILL LEVEL: DIFFICULT

SIZE

TO FIT AN AVERAGE ADULT CAT

- EAR OPENING: 6 CM (2½ IN.)
- WIDTH OF HAT BETWEEN EARS: 6 CM (2½ IN.)

SUPPLIES

- 27 M (30 YD) ARAN WEIGHT YARN IN A (YELLOW)
- 9 M (10 YD) ARAN WEIGHT YARN IN B (WHITE)
- 9 M (10 YD) ARAN WEIGHT YARN IN C (ORANGE)
- 4 MM CROCHET HOOK
- YARN NEEDLE
- POLYESTER FIBRE FILLING

BASE

Using yarn A, work 2ch, leaving a 64 cm (25 in.) tail.

Row 1: 3dc in 2nd ch, 1ch.
Row 2: 3dc, 1ch.
Row 3: 2dc in first st, 1dc, 2dc in last st, 1ch. (5dc)
Row 4: 5dc, 1ch.
Row 5: 2dc in first st, 3dc, 2dc in last st, 1ch. (7dc)
Row 6: 7dc, 1ch.
Row 7: 2dc in first st, 5dc, 2dc in last st, 1ch. (9dc)
Row 8: 9dc, 1ch.
Row 9: 2dc in first st, 7dc, 2dc in last st, 1ch. (11dc)
Row 10: 11dc, 1ch.
Row 11: 2dc in first st, 9dc, 2dc in last st, 1ch. (13dc)

FIRST EAR HOLE

Row 12: 1dc, 11ch, 1dc in last st, 1ch.

MIDDLE SECTION

Rows 13–22: 13dc, 1ch.

SECOND EAR HOLE

Row 23: 1dc, 11ch, 1dc in last st, 1ch.
Row 24: 13dc, 1ch.
Row 25: 1dc, skip next st, 9dc, skip next st, 1dc, 1ch. (11dc)
Row 26: 11dc, 1ch.
Row 27: 1dc, skip next st, 7dc, skip next st, 1dc, 1ch. (9dc)
Row 28: 9dc, 1ch.
Row 29: 1dc, skip next st, 5dc, skip next st, 1dc, 1ch. (7dc)
Row 30: 7dc, 1ch.
Row 31: 1dc, skip next st, 3dc, skip next st, 1dc, 1ch. (5dc)
Row 32: 5dc, 1ch.
Row 33: 1dc, skip next st, 1dc, skip next st, 1dc, 1ch. (3dc)
Row 34: 3dc, 1ch.
Row 35: 1dc in last st.

To create ties, work 25ch, snip yarn and pull through loop tightly. Trim tail. Work 25ch at beg of base, using 64 cm (25 in.) tail.

TRAFFIC CONE

Using yarn B, make a magic ring.
Rnd 1: 1ch, 6dc in ring.
Rnd 2: 6dc.
Rnd 3: [2dc in next st, 2dc] twice. (8dc)
Rnds 4–5: Dc around.
Rnd 6: [2dc in next st, 3dc] twice. (10dc)
Rnds 7–8: Dc around.
Rnd 9: [2dc in next st, 4dc] twice. (12dc)
Change to yarn C.
Rnds 10–11: Dc around.
Rnd 12: [2dc in next st, 5dc] twice. (14dc)
Rnds 13–14: Dc around.
Rnd 15: [2dc in next st, 6dc] twice. (16dc)

Rnds 16–17: Dc around.
Rnd 18: [2dc in next st, 7dc] twice. (18dc)

Cut yarn, leaving a 38 cm (15 in.) tail, and pull through loop. Turn hat inside out. Sew yarn B tail to close up top gap. Weave ends to inside and finish.

ASSEMBLY

Lightly and evenly stuff traffic cone with polyester fibre filling. Be careful to maintain a soft square point at the top of the cone. Stitch hat onto the centre of the base with yarn C tail, with the square top facing towards the front (not the ears) of the hat. Use the photos if necessary for reference. Secure ends to underside of base and finish.

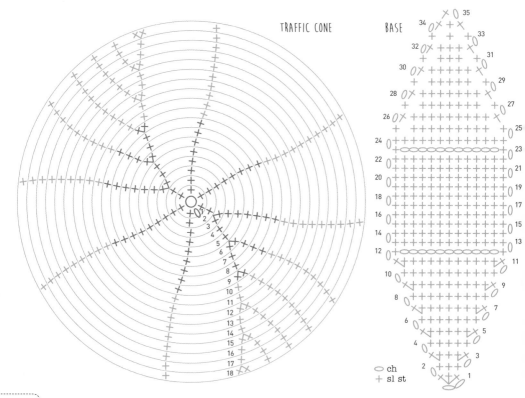

TRAFFIC CONE

BASE

○ ch
+ sl st

SIZE

TO FIT AN AVERAGE
ADULT CAT

- EAR OPENING: 5 CM (2 IN.)
- WIDTH OF HAT BETWEEN
  EARS: 6 CM (2½ IN.)

SUPPLIES

- 19 M (21 YD) ARAN
  WEIGHT YARN IN A
  (PURPLE)
- 9 M (10 YD) ARAN WEIGHT
  YARN IN B (BLUE)
- 4 MM CROCHET HOOK
- YARN NEEDLE
- POLYESTER FIBRE FILLING

GUS LOOKS
ENCHANTING IN
HIS UNICORN HAT.

ONCE EXTINCT, THE RARE UNICORN CAT GRACES ONLY
THE MOST FANTASTICAL OF HOMES. ADD A BRIGHTLY
COLOURED FRINGE MANE ALONG THE TOP OF THE HAT
FOR A LITTLE FLAIR!

UNICORN

HORN: 5 CM
(2 IN.) HIGH

BASE

Using yarn A, work 2ch,
leaving a 7.5 cm (3 in.) tail.
Row 1: 3dc in 2nd ch, 1ch.
Row 2: 3dc, 1ch.
Row 3: 2dc in first st, 1dc, 2dc
in last st, 1ch. (5dc)
Row 4: 5dc, 1ch.
Row 5: 2dc in first st, 3dc, 2dc
in last st, 1ch. (7dc)
Row 6: 7dc, 1ch.
Row 7: 2dc in first st, 5dc, 2dc in
last st, 1ch. (9dc)
Row 8: 9dc, 1ch.
Row 9: 2dc in first st, 7dc, 2dc in last
st, 1ch. (11dc)
Row 10: 11dc, 1ch.
Row 11: 2dc in first st, 9dc, 2dc in last st,
1ch. (13dc)
FIRST EAR HOLE
Row 12: 1dc, 11ch, 1dc in last st, 1ch.
MIDDLE SECTION
Rows 13–22: 13dc, 1ch.
SECOND EAR HOLE
Row 23: 1dc, 11ch, 1dc in last st, 1ch.
Row 24: 13dc, 1ch.
Row 25: 1dc, skip next st, 9dc, skip next st, 1dc,
1ch. (11dc)
Row 26: 11dc, 1ch.
Row 27: 1dc, skip next st, 7dc, skip next st, 1dc,
1ch. (9dc)

Row 28: 9dc, 1ch.

Row 29: 1dc, skip next st, 5dc, skip next st, 1dc, 1ch. (7dc)

Row 30: 7dc, 1ch.

Row 31: 1dc, skip next st, 3dc, skip next st, 1dc, 1ch. (5dc)

Row 32: 5dc, 1ch.

Row 33: 1dc, skip next st, 1dc, skip next st, 1dc, 1ch. (3dc)

Row 34: 3dc, 1ch.

Row 35: 1dc in last st.

Cut yarn, leaving a 7.5 cm (3 in.) tail. Weave in both tails to underside of base.

UNICORN HORN

Using yarn B, make a magic ring.

Rnd 1: 1ch, 4dc in ring.

Rnd 2: Dc in each st around, sl st in first dc. (4dc)

Rnd 3: [2dc in next st, 1dc] twice. (6dc)

Rnd 4: Dc around.

Rnd 5: [2dc in next st, 2dc] twice. (8dc)

Rnd 6: Dc around.

Rnd 7: [2dc in next st, 3dc] twice. (10dc)

Rnd 8: Dc around.

Rnd 9: [2dc in next st, 4dc] twice. (12dc)

Rnd 10: Dc around.

Rnd 11: [2dc in next st, 5dc] twice. (14dc)

Rnd 12: Dc around.

Cut yarn, leaving a 38 cm (15 in.) tail, and pull through loop tightly.

ASSEMBLY

Weave in tail from top of unicorn horn, making sure to close any gaps. Lightly stuff horn with polyester fibre filling, making sure to stuff evenly. Using 38 cm (15 in.) tail, securely stitch horn to the centre of the base, close to front of hat.

Using yarn B, measure out two pieces of yarn 64 cm (25 in.) each. To create ties at each end of the base, use one piece of yarn and pull a loop through the end of the hat, work 25ch, pull yarn through loop tightly and snip. Repeat with other piece on the other side of the hat.

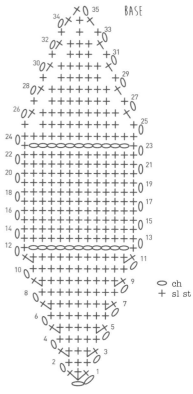

BASE

○ ch
+ sl st

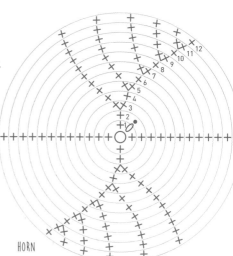

HORN

METHOD: CROCHET

SKILL LEVEL: DIFFICULT

SIZE

TO FIT AN AVERAGE
ADULT CAT

- LENGTH: 13 CM (5 IN.)
- WIDTH: 7.5 CM (3 IN.)

✳ ✳ ✳ ✳ ✳

SUPPLIES

- 37 M (40 YD) ARAN
  WEIGHT YARN IN A
  (BEIGE)
- 5.5 M (6 YD) ARAN
  WEIGHT YARN IN B (BLUE)
- 5.5 M (6 YD) ARAN
  WEIGHT YARN IN C
  (ORANGE)
- 3.5 MM CROCHET HOOK
- YARN NEEDLE

TRANSPORT YOUR CAT TO THE WILD WEST IN THIS PERFECTLY BROKEN-IN COWBOY HAT!

COWBOY HAT

HAT

Do not turn work in this pattern.
Using yarn A, work 6ch.
Rnd 1: 2dc in 2nd ch, 1dc in next 3ch, 3dc in next ch.
Continuing along other side of chain, work 1dc in back loop
of next 4ch, sl st to beg ch, 1ch. (12 sts)
Rnd 2: 1dc in first st, 2dc in next st, 4dc, [2dc in next st]
twice, 4dc, sl st to beg ch, 1ch. (15sts)
Rnd 3: 2dc in next 2sts, 5dc, 2dc in next 2sts, sl st to next dc;
this marks new position for start of rnd. (This will cause the
hat to start to curl, which is part of the shaping.)
For the following rnds, use a marker at the beg of each rnd to
help keep your place. On Rnds 4–13 inclusive, work 1ch at beg
of each rnd and end each rnd with sl st to beg ch.
Rnd 4: [5dc, 2dc in next st] 4 times.
Rnd 5: [6dc, 2dc in next st] 4 times.
Rnd 6: [7dc, 2dc in next st] 4 times.
Rnd 7: [8dc, 2dc in next st] 4 times.
Rnd 8: [9dc, 2dc in next st] 4 times.
Rnd 9: [10dc, 2dc in next st] 4 times.
Rnds 10–12: Dc around.
BRIM
Rnd 13: 2dc in each st around, sl st to beg ch.
Rnd 14: Sl st in each st around.
Snip yarn, leaving enough tail to weave in ends.

TO SHAPE

You have created two points at the top of your hat.
These points should face the ears, and you should
use the starting tail to stitch into place a dip in between
these points. You may find it helpful to turn to the WS,
or inside, of the hat and, pinching between the points,
secure this shape with a few stitches.

Turning to the RS, or outside, of the hat, you will need to stitch your brim into place. You want the sides of the hat to roll. Lightly roll each side and work 3 or 4 stitches to hold it in place. Use the photos for reference. Properly broken in hats have an authentic shape, which means you don't have to perfectly stitch the brim rolls. Just remember that the front and back need to be flat. Stitching the brim is what gives the hat its final shape, so adjust it according to your liking. An experienced crocheter could give this hat a stiffer shape by stuffing it. You would need to crochet an oval, or small base, to stitch your hat onto and to hold the stuffing in. You could use the other patterns in this book as a reference for this if you wish.

TIES
(Make 2)
Using a strand of all three yarn colours, make two braided ties that each measure 90 cm (1 yd). You could also use a 0.5 cm (¼ in.) wide ribbon or trim of your choice for ties.

To attach ties to the hat, take one tie and pull it through the front left side (near the rolled brim) of the hat. Use a larger crochet hook if necessary. Now pull the other end of the tie through the front right side of the hat (again near the rolled brim). Repeat with other tie at the back of the hat. Use the photos for reference if necessary.

TO WEAR
You now have 4 ties hanging underneath your hat, two on the right and two on the left. Carefully tie the two left and the two right ties together in a bow under the chin. Make sure the ties are on either side of the ear on each side. This ensures a more comfortable fit (your cat's ears should be clear of the hat). If you need the hat to be a bit smaller or larger on top, adjust the roll of the brim.

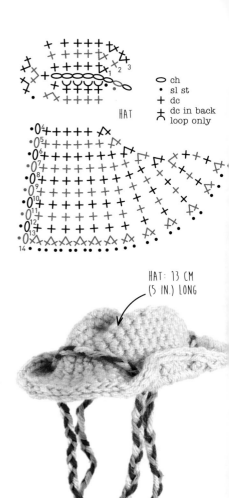

HAT

○ ch
• sl st
+ dc
⊥ dc in back loop only

HAT: 13 CM (5 IN.) LONG

TIES: BRAID 3 COLOURS TOGETHER

YEE-HAW! BLUEBELL IS THE
NEW COWBOY IN TOWN!

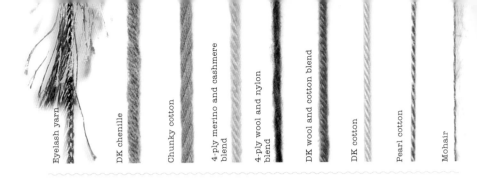

Eyelash yarn

DK chenille

Chunky cotton

4-ply merino and cashmere blend

4-ply wool and nylon blend

DK wool and cotton blend

DK cotton

Pearl cotton

Mohair

MATERIALS AND EQUIPMENT

THE NEAT THING ABOUT MAKING CAT HATS IS THAT THEY DON'T REQUIRE SPECIALIST TOOLS, NOR DO THEY USE MUCH YARN.

YARNS

Yarns are available in a range of weights, from very fine to super chunky. Because yarns may vary from one manufacturer to another and certainly change from one fibre to another, only generic yarn types are indicated for the hats in this book. You should be aware of the properties of different yarns, however, from the fullness of cotton to the elasticity of wool, because the construction of a yarn will affect its behaviour and characteristics, and so will influence the end result. Try using different yarns and, if in doubt, use a smaller needle/hook size than usual. Separate your yarns into colour groups and keep these in transparent plastic containers so that you have a palette of colours to work with.

KNITTING NEEDLES

Needle sizes are specified for each hat. Pairs of knitting needles are made in a variety of lengths. Most are aluminium, although larger-size needles are made of plastic to reduce their weight. For most of the designs in this book, a conventional pair of needles is used, but double-pointed needles are used in some of the projects.

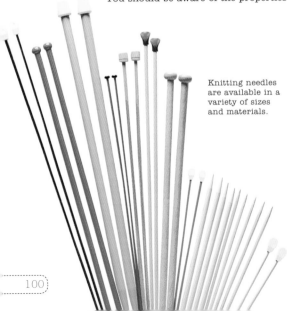

Knitting needles are available in a variety of sizes and materials.

CROCHET HOOKS

Crochet hooks are available in a wide range of sizes and materials. Most hooks are made from aluminium or plastic. Small sizes of steel hooks are made for working with very fine yarns. Handmade wooden, bamboo and horn hooks are also available.

Hook sizes are quoted differently in Europe and the United States, and some brands of hook are labelled with more than one numbering system. Choosing a hook is largely a matter of personal preference. The design of the hook affects the ease of working considerably. Look for a hook that has a comfortable grip.

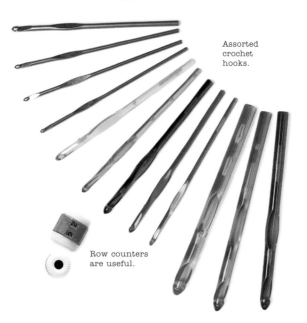

Assorted crochet hooks.

Row counters are useful.

STUFFING MATERIALS AND ADDITIONAL EQUIPMENT

POLYESTER FIBRE FILLING

There are a number of options open to you when it comes to stuffing your hat, including foam, cotton wadding and polyester fibre filling. I recommend polyester fibre filling, a synthetic fibre that is extremely lightweight and also washable. It has a soft feel and it bounces back into shape. It tends to clump less than many of the other stuffing materials. It is also widely available.

TAPE MEASURE

Essential for measuring lengths of yarn, choose one that features both centimetres and inches on the same side.

MARKERS AND ROW COUNTERS

Ready-made markers can be used to indicate a repeat or to help count stitches in a chain. Similarly, a row counter may help you to keep track of the number of rows you have worked, but in knitting this is usually easy if you remember to include the stitches on the needle as a row.

Always have a sharp pair of scissors handy.

A tape measure lets you check that you have adequate yarn.

KNITTING TECHNIQUES

HERE IS A REMINDER OF THE BASICS, TOGETHER WITH A FEW SUGGESTSIONS AND TECHNIQUES THAT MIGHT BE NEW TO A BEGINNING KNITTER.

SLIPKNOT

1 Putting a slipknot on the needle makes the first stitch of the cast on. Loop the yarn around two fingers of the left hand, the ball end on top. Dip the needle into the loop, catch the ball end of the yarn and pull it through the loop.

2 Pull the ends of the yarn to tighten the knot. Tighten the ball end to bring the knot up to the needle.

CASTING ON

There are several cast on methods, each with its own merits.

Thumb method

Sometimes called long-tail cast on, this uses a single needle and produces an elastic edge.

1 Leaving an end about three times the length of the required cast on, put a slipknot on the needle. Holding the yarn end in the left hand, take the left thumb under the yarn and upwards. Insert the needle in the loop made on the thumb.

2 Use the ball end of the yarn to make a knit stitch, slipping the loop off the thumb. Pull the yarn end to close the stitch up to the needle. Continue making stitches in this way. The result looks like a row of garter stitch because the yarn has been knitted off the thumb.

Cable cast on

This two-needle method gives a firm edge with the appearance of a rope.

1 Put a slipknot on one needle. Use the other needle and the ball end of the yarn to knit into the loop on the left-hand needle without slipping it off. Transfer the new stitch to the left-hand needle.

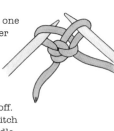

2 Insert the right-hand needle between the new stitch and the next stitch, and then make another stitch as before. Continue making stitches in this way.

Knitted cast on

Make a cable cast on as above, but instead of knitting between stitches, insert the right-hand needle in the front of each stitch in the usual way. This gives a softer edge than the cable method.

I-CORD

A very useful round cord can be made using two double-pointed needles. Cast on four (or the required number of) stitches and knit one row in the usual way. *Without turning, slide the stitches to the opposite end of the needle. Take the yarn firmly across the wrong side from left to right and knit one row. Repeat from * for the required length.

CASTING OFF

A simple knit stitch cast off is used in this book. Knit two stitches. *With the left needle, lift the first stitch over the second and off the right needle. Knit the next stitch. Repeat from * until one stitch remains. Break off the yarn, pass the end through this stitch and tighten.

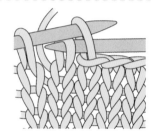

PICK UP AND KNIT

The pick up and knit technique involves knitting up new stitches along the edge of a knitted piece, ready to work in another direction. This avoids having to cast on a separate piece and join it with a seam. With RS facing you, insert the right needle under an edge stitch, take the yarn around the needle and pull a loop through to make a stitch. Repeat for the number of stitches required, spacing the picked up stitches evenly along the edge. The next row will be a WS row.

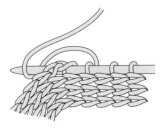

KNITTING IN THE ROUND

When knitting in the round using four double-pointed needles (dpns), the stitches are distributed among three of the needles and the spare needle is used to knit with. Bring the first and third needles together to form a circle and use the spare needle to work the stitches off the first (left) needle and onto the spare (right) needle in the usual way. This is done with the RS (outside) of the work facing you, unless stated otherwise. Take the yarn firmly from one double-pointed needle to the next or a ladder will appear.

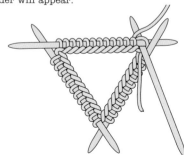

CROCHET TECHNIQUES

HERE ARE A FEW REMINDERS OF THE BASICS AND SOME SUGGESTIONS FOR BUILDING ON THEM.

SLIPKNOT

1 Putting a slipknot on the hook makes the first loop of the chain that will hold the stitches of the first row or round. Loop the yarn around two fingers of the left hand, the ball end to the front. Insert the hook in the loop, catch the ball end of the yarn and pull it through the loop.

2 Pull the ends of yarn to tighten the knot. Now tighten the ball end to bring the knot up to the hook.

HOOKING ACTION

Hold the slipknot (and later the chain) between the thumb and forefinger of the left hand. Take the yarn over the second finger of the left hand so it is held taut. Take it around the little finger as well if necessary. The right hand is then free to manipulate the hook. With a turn of the wrist, guide the tip of the hook under the yarn. Catch the yarn and pull it through the loop on the hook to make a chain.

Hooking and catching is referred to as yarn over hook (abbreviation: yo). It is the action used in making a chain, a slip stitch and, in various combinations, all other crochet stitches.

Note Unless the instructions state otherwise, the hook should be inserted under the two strands of yarn that form the top of the chain, or the top of the stitch.

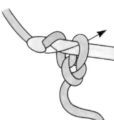

WORKING A SLIP STITCH (SL ST)

Slip stitch is the shortest of all the crochet stitches and its main uses are for joining rounds, making seams and carrying the hook and yarn from one place to another. Insert the hook from front to back into the required stitch. Wrap the yarn over the hook (yarn over) and draw it through both the work and the loop on the hook. One loop remains on the hook and one slip stitch has been worked.

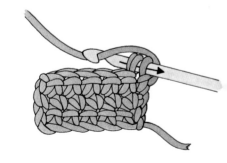

CHAIN RING

Join a number of chain stitches into a ring with a slip stitch in the first chain. Work the first round of stitches around the chain and into the centre of the ring. If the yarn end is also worked around, the ring is lightly padded and this end can be pulled to tighten it.

MAGIC RING

1 To make a magic ring, first coil the yarn around two fingers and then use the hook to pull through a loop of the ball end of the yarn, as if making a slipknot (see step 1, far left). However, do not then pull the yarn tight. Holding the ring flat between the thumb and forefinger of the left hand, catch the yarn and pull it through the loop on the hook to anchor it.

2 Working under two strands of yarn each time, make the stitches as directed and then pull the free yarn end to close the ring. Join the ring with a slip stitch in the first stitch.

JOINING IN A NEW YARN

There are several methods you can use to join in a new yarn or colour.

Using slip stitch

This method can be used when working any stitch. Make a slipknot in the new yarn and place it on the hook. Insert the hook into the work at the specified position and make a slip stitch with the new yarn through

both stitch and slipknot. Continue working the pattern with the new yarn.

Changing colours mid-stitch

To switch neatly from an old colour to a new colour in the same place, you can leave the last stitch in the old colour incomplete and use the new colour to finish the stitch.

1 Using the old colour, leave the last stage of the final stitch incomplete, so that there are two loops on the hook. Wrap the new colour over the hook and pull it through the loops on the hook to complete the stitch.

2 Continue working with the new colour. You may find it easier to knot the two loose ends together before you cut the yarn no longer in use, leaving ends of about 10 cm (4 in.). Always undo the knot before weaving in the yarn ends.

ADDITIONAL TECHNIQUES

ALL THE HATS ARE EASY TO ASSEMBLE USING JUST A FEW STANDARD
FINISHING TECHNIQUES. HERE ARE SOME TIPS AND SUGGESTIONS.

MARKERS

If markers are needed to count rows or
repeats, use a length of contrast thread.
*Lay it between stitches from front to back,
make a stitch and then bring it from back
to front of the work. Repeat from * once
more. It can be pulled out when it is no
longer needed.

STUFFING

Use synthetic toy stuffing such as polyester
fibre filling rather than cotton wool, as the
latter can be rather dense and difficult to
stitch through. Push the stuffing in firmly,
one wisp at a time, using it to shape the
object without distorting it. Too much
stuffing will pack down, whereas too little
will never plump up. Don't push the stuffing
in with a pointed implement, but use
something like the eraser end of a pencil.
Spare matching yarn may be better than
polyester fibre filling inside crochet, as
there will be no show-through. Wind off
short lengths of yarn around two fingers
and push these in, one coil at a time.

ENDS

Sometimes called a tail, the end of yarn
left after making the slipknot should be
a reasonable length so that it can be used
for sewing up. It can also be very useful
for covering up imperfections, such as
awkward colour changes. The same applies
to the end left after casting or fastening
off. In these projects, ends that will not
be needed for sewing up should be woven
in and secured to the WS before the main
assembly of the hat.

POMPOMS

A couple of the hats in this book require pompoms. Either use a
ready-made plastic pompom maker or cut out two rings of cardboard.

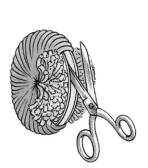
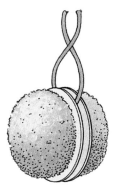

1 Place the two rings together
and use a yarn needle to wrap
yarn around them.

2 Starting new lengths of
yarn at the outside edge,
continue until the rings are
tightly covered. Insert the
blade of a pair of scissors
between the rings and cut
the yarn around the edge.

3 Tie a length of yarn around
the pompom between the
rings. Knot the yarn tightly,
slip the rings off and trim
the pompom. Use the ends of
yarn from the tie for attaching
the pompom to the hat.

JOINING KNITTED AND CROCHETED PIECES

It is always best to leave a lengthy tail when you cast
on or cast off, as this tail can serve as your joining
yarn when sewing pieces together. The projects in this
book specify at which point to leave additional length.
Carefully place the piece to be attached in the correct
location, pinning it in place if necessary. Using a blunt
yarn needle and the tail (or a length of matching yarn),
stitch small upright stitches through the edge of the
piece being joined to the main piece of the project.
When done in the same shade of yarn, these stitches
should be invisible. Once attached, pull the yarn to the
wrong side of the knitted or crocheted object (usually
the underside of the hat) and secure with several
knots. Weave in ends.

ABBREVIATIONS

GENERAL

rep   repeat

rnd(s) round(s)

RS   right side(s)

st(s)   stitch(es)

WS   wrong side(s)

KNITTING

dpn(s) double-pointed needle(s)

k   knit

k2tog knit two stitches together

kfb   knit into front and back of stitch to make two stitches from one

p   purl

CROCHET

beg   beginning

ch   chain

dc   double crochet

sl st   slip stitch

sp   space

yo   yarn forward and over hook to make a stitch

READING CHARTS

Each crochet design is accompanied by a chart that should be read with the written instructions.

The chart represents the right side of the work.

CHARTS IN ROWS

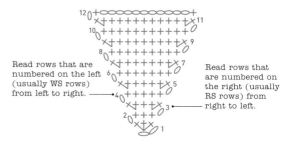

Read rows that are numbered on the left (usually WS rows) from left to right.

Read rows that are numbered on the right (usually RS rows) from right to left.

CHARTS IN ROUNDS

Charts for working in the round begin at the centre and are read anticlockwise (in the same direction as working).

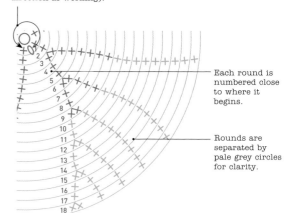

Each round is numbered close to where it begins.

Rounds are separated by pale grey circles for clarity.

YARNS USED

Many thanks to Lion Brand who generously supplied the yarn used in this book.

The following yarns and colours were used for the hats:

Dinosaur, pages 10–13
A: Jiffy, Avocado
B: Wool Ease, Pumpkin

Bobble Hat, pages 14–15
A: Wool Ease, Seaspray
B: Wool Ease, Cranberry

Strawberry, pages 16–19
A: Cotton Ease, Cherry
B: Kitchen Cotton, Snap Pea
C: Cotton Ease, Snow

Pumpkin, pages 20–21
A: Kitchen Cotton, Pumpkin
B: Cotton Ease, Lime

Sports Cap, pages 22–23
A: Wool Ease, Ranch Red
B: Vanna's Choice, White
C: Wool Ease, Sea Spray

Spring Chick, pages 24–25
A: Romance, Passion
B: Fun Yarn, Black
C: Kitchen Cotton, Pumpkin

Punk Mohawk, pages 26–29
A: Vanna's Choice, Black
B: Roving Wool, Hot Pink

Bunny, pages 30–31
Nature's Choice Organic Cotton, Almond

Turkey, pages 32–35
A: Jiffy, Caffe
B: Fun Yarn, Red
C: Fun Yarn, Black
D: Kitchen Cotton, Pumpkin
E: Wool Ease, Fisherman

Flower Cap, pages 36–37
A: Kitchen Cotton, Cayenne
B: Wool Ease, Blue Heather

I Heart You, pages 38–39
A: Jiffy, Caffe
B: Jiffy, Chili

Extraterrestrial, pages 40–41
A: Vanna's Choice, Sweet Pea
B: Vanna's Choice, Black

Antlers, pages 42–43
Jiffy, Caffe

Party Hat, pages 44–45
A: Vanna's Choice, Raspberry
B: Wool Ease, Fisherman
C: Vanna's Choice, Mint

Witch, pages 46–47
A: Kitchen Cotton, Grape
B: Kitchen Cotton, Snap Pea

Cupcake, pages 48–49
A: Vanna's Choice, Pink Poodle
B: Vanna's Choice, Berrylicious
C: Vanna's Choice, Angel White

Banana, pages 50–51
A: Baby's First, Honeybee
B: Wool Ease, Cocoa

Santa Hat, pages 52–55
A: Jiffy, Chili
B: Jiffy, White

Elf, pages 56–57
A: Jiffy, Apple
B: Jiffy, Chili

Top Hat, pages 58–61
A: Fun Yarn, Black
B: Vanna's Glamour, Moonstone

Pompom Hat, pages 62–63
A: Vanna's Choice, Raspberry
B: Vanna's Choice, Fern

Little Lion, pages 64–67
A: Vanna's Choice, Honey
B: Wool Ease, Paprika

Feline Fox, pages 68–71
A: Wool Ease, Paprika
B: Wool Ease, Fisherman
C: Fun Yarn, Black

Baby Bear, pages 72–75
A: Heartland Yarn, Big Bend
B: Wool Ease, Fisherman

Dog, pages 76–79
A: Wool Ease, Fisherman
B: Heartland Yarn, Big Bend

Shark Attack, pages 80–83
A: Kitchen Cotton, Tropic Breeze
B: Kitchen Cotton, Red
C: Kitchen Cotton, Vanilla

Santa Paws, pages 84–87
A: Vanna's Choice, Scarlet
B: Vanna's Choice, White

Traffic Cone, pages 88–91
A: Kitchen Cotton, Citrus
B: Kitchen Cotton, Vanilla
C: Kitchen Cotton, Pumpkin

Unicorn, pages 92–95
A: Vanna's Choice, Dusty Purple
B: Vanna's Choice, Aqua

Cowboy Hat, pages 96–99
A: Vanna's Choice, Beige
B: Kitchen Cotton, Tropic Breeze
C: Wool Ease, Paprika

INDEX

B

Baby Bear 72–75
Banana 50–51
Bobble Hat 14–15
Bunny 30–31

C

casting off 103
casting on 102
   cable cast on 102
   knitted cast on 102
   thumb method 102
Cowboy Hat 96–99
crochet hooks 101
Cupcake 48–49

D

Dinosaur 10–13
Dog 76–79

E

Elf 56–57
equipment 100–101
Extraterrestrial 40–41

F

fastening off 103
Feline Fox 68–71
fibre filling 101, 106
Flower Cap 36–37

I

i-cord 103
I Heart You 38–39

K

knitting needles 100
knitting techniques 102–103
   casting off 103
   casting on 102
   i-cord 103
   knitting in the round 103
   pick up and knit 103
   slipknots 102

L

Little Lion 64–67

M

markers 101
materials 100–101

P

Party Hat 44–45
pick up and knit 103
polyester fibre filling 101, 106
Pompom Hat 62–63
Pumpkin 20–21
Punk Mohawk 26–29

R

Reindeer Antlers 42–43
row counters 101

S

Santa Hat 52–55
Santa Paws 84–87
scissors 101
Shark Attack 80–83
slipknots 102
Sports Cap 22–23
Spring Chick 24–25
Strawberry 16–19

T

tape measures 101
Top Hat 58–61
Traffic Cone 88–91
Turkey 32–35

U

Unicorn 92–95

W

Witch 46–47

Y

yarns 100

STARRING

Many thanks to our feline friends and their families for appearing in this book:

Anna Nicole (black-and-white domestic shorthair), courtesy of Sophie Bremaud, featured on pages 80–83

Bluebell (grey Selkirk Rex), courtesy of Alison Hayward, featured on pages 96–99

Daisy (black-and-white domestic shorthair), courtesy of Simon Baker, featured on page 55

Domino (black-and-white domestic longhair), courtesy of Wendie Cattell, featured on pages 68–69, 76–79

Gracie (Maine Coon), courtesy of Clare Earthy, featured on pages 24

Gus (grey domestic shorthair), courtesy of Leah Prado, featured on pages 16–19, 41, 50, 92–93

Holly (Maine Coon), courtesy of Clare Earthy, featured on pages 30, 91

Huck (Maine Coon), courtesy of Clare Earthy, featured on pages 31, 53, 95

Jasper (chocolate domestic longhair), courtesy of Katherine Shone, featured on pages 26–29, 42r

Jess (domestic longhair), courtesy of Wendy Cattell, featured on pages 88–89

Leeroy (lilac straight-eared Scottish Fold), courtesy of Joanna Bettles, featured on pages 10–13, 20–21, 49

Link (blue-point Birman), courtesy of Rozi Blair, featured on pages 37, 46–47, 52

Luna (Snow Bengal cross), courtesy of Alix Taylor, featured on pages 14–15, 22–23

Lyric (blue-point Birman), courtesy of Rozi Blair, featured on pages 32–34, 36–37

Mooch (British Shorthair with Siamese points), courtesy of Simone Hogan, featured on pages 45, 58–61, 62, 84, 86

Percy (ginger-and-white domestic shorthair), courtesy of Katherine Shone, featured on pages 38–39, 42l

Poppy (tabby domestic shorthair), courtesy of Simon Baker, featured on pages 64–67, 85

Rachel (black-and-white domestic shorthair), courtesy of Wendie Cattell, featured on page 63

Vivi (red-silver Abyssinian), courtesy of Alix Taylor, featured on pages 56, 72–75

And many thanks to the photographers, Liz Coleman and Phil Wilkins, for their patience, ingenuity, and creativity.